Food of the World
INDIA

BEVERLY LEBLANC

Food of the World
INDIA

p

This is a Parragon Publishing Book
First published in 2004

Parragon Publishing
Queen Street House
4 Queen Street
Bath, BA1 1HE, United Kingdom

Created and produced by The Bridgewater Book Company Ltd.
Project Editor Emily Casey Bailey
Project Designer Michael Whitehead
Photography David Jordan
Editor Kay Halsey
Home Economist Jacqui Bellefontaine
Additional photography Max Alexander (11, 15, 22, 78, 80, 96, 124, 144, 151,
196, 206, 208, 228), Adrian Bailey (100, 109, 141, 156, 203, 212, 214, 232),
Jonathan Bailey (48, 52, 59, 68, 103, 239, 240, 249, 250), Caroline Jones
(2, 12, 17, 18, 20, 25, 35, 36, 56, 169, 171, 172, 189, 198, 224, 231)

ISBN: 1-40543-364-7

Printed in Indonesia

NOTES FOR THE READER

• This book uses imperial, metric, or US cup measurements. Follow the same units
  of measurement throughout; do not mix imperial and metric.

• All spoon measurements are level: teaspoons are assumed to be 5 ml, and tablespoons
  are assumed to be 15 ml.

• Unless otherwise stated, milk is assumed to be whole, eggs and individual vegetables
  such as potatoes are medium, and pepper is freshly ground black pepper.

• Recipes using raw or very lightly cooked eggs should be avoided by infants, the
  elderly, pregnant women, convalescents, and anyone suffering from an illness.

• The times given are an approximate guide only. Preparation times differ according
  to the techniques used by different people and the cooking times may also vary
  from those given.

contents

INTRODUCTION

10 Indian food is as vibrant, colorful, and intriguing as the country itself. The numerous and diverse regional cuisines reflect the sheer massive size of India, its huge population, its history as a trading and occupied nation, and, of course, the mix of ancient religions that are practiced. India's culinary traditions have been born out of great wealth and great poverty, and offer exciting flavors unlike anywhere else on Earth.

The Indian subcontinent covers about 1.3 million square miles, stretching over 1,800 miles from the snow-capped, towering peaks of the Himalayas southward to the tropical plains of Tamil Nadu, bordered by the Malabar and Coromandel coasts with their elegant coconut palms. Wheat and other grains thrive in the fertile northern lands irrigated by the Ganges and Indus rivers, while rice also grows in the southern coastal regions, providing the two staple ingredients for the more than one billion Indians.

Indian cooks also utilize fish and shellfish from more than 3,700 miles of coastline along the Arabian Sea and the Bay of Bengal, as well as numerous inland lakes, rivers, and waterways. Fruits and vegetables are grown throughout the country, as well as numerous lentils, beans, and peas that help sustain millions of vegetarians. Sprawling spice plantations in southern India provide the flavors that make the food unique.

It's impossible to appreciate the complexity of Indian food without considering the influence of the established religions, each of which has different dietary laws. Although Westerners can read about how the cow is sacred in India, what this means in practice only becomes apparent after observing traffic in cosmopolitan Delhi grind to a halt as a cow strolls across the street. Religion touches all aspects of secular life in India, which naturally includes food and eating customs.

Although the overwhelming majority of India's population is Hindu, the other established religions include Islam, Buddhism, Judaism, Christianity, and Zoroastrianism, the Parsis' religion. This mix throws up numerous considerations for Indian cooks, or anyone cooking for Indians. Some Hindus and Sikhs are vegetarians, yet others eat all meats, except beef, and there aren't any restrictions on consuming dairy products made from cows' and water buffaloes' milk. Muslims don't eat pork. Kosher Jews don't touch pork or shellfish. Christians and Parsis eat meat, poultry, seafood, and vegetables. Buddhists and Jains are strict vegetarians, with Jains even excluding all root vegetables, garlic, and onion from their diets. Add to these religious taboos the fact that meat is too expensive for millions upon millions of Indians, and the result is the exciting cuisine of India, which includes an unrivaled range of vegetarian dishes.

Religion and food are also intertwined in the numerous religious festivals that dot the calendar year. The Hindu festival of lights, Divali, when Laxmi, the goddess of wealth, is prayed to, includes eating many sweetmeats while visiting families and friends. Ramadan is the Muslim month of sunrise-to-sunset fasting, and each night the fast is broken with a large

Boats drift lazily along the palm-fringed backwaters of Kerala in India's southernmost state

feast. Christians feast at Christmas on roast suckling pig and distribute marzipan candy, while dishes such as fish fillets in a cherry tomato sauce are served at most Parsi religious festivals and weddings.

Small portions of food, such as rice or coconut in the south and small sweet milk cakes in the north, are offered with prayers to images of specific gods in Hindu homes. After the food has been blessed, a small amount of the offering is eaten in the belief that the prayers will be granted.

Indian culinary history has also been shaped by numerous outside influences. After several attempts, the Muslim Moghuls successfully invaded northern India from Persia in the sixteenth century, establishing a dynasty that lasted almost 200 years. As part of the Moghuls' sophisticated lifestyle—rich in music, elegant and tranquil gardens, beautiful architecture, and exquisite fabrics—they introduced a highly refined style of cooking. Written accounts of the lavish feasts and banquets record generous hospitality and great extravagance. The Moghul tradition of using fresh and dried fruits, nuts, meat, exotic spices such as saffron and cardamom, and rich cream sauces continues today in the biryanis, pilafs, pasandas, and kormas that are still appreciated around the world.

By the time Moghul power ended in the eighteenth century, European intervention and territory acquisition had already begun, adding another dimension to India's culinary history. The Portuguese, for example, desperate to control the lucrative Indian spice trade, had captured Goa, off the west coast. This gave Christianity a foothold on the subcontinent, but more importantly from the perspective of the kitchen, the Portuguese troops introduced the chili pepper, perhaps the most common flavoring used today.

Wooden string puppets made by skilled craftspeople are a traditional artform in western India

The Moghuls introduced a highly refined style of cooking

Although the Dutch and French also established trading posts, the dominating foreign force became the British East India Company, which eventually led to the establishment of the British Raj. Its lasting culinary legacy is in the Anglo-Indian kitchens, primarily around Kolkata, known as Calcutta at the time of British rule. It was also in part due to the constant travels to and from Britain that the exciting flavors of India became well known and appreciated abroad.

Indian food abroad

Indian food is popular around the world, particularly in areas of Indian immigration, and at the start of the twenty-first century, Chicken Tikka Masala (see page 161) continually tops all opinion polls of the most popular Asian dishes, though its Indian heritage is somewhat suspect.

Punjabi and Bangladeshi chefs and restaurateurs are credited with spreading the enthusiasm for Indian food, especially in Britain, opening numerous neighborhood restaurants in the years since Partition in 1947. And it was the Punjabi formula of serving tandoori-style recipes from home along with rich Moghul-inspired meat and rice dishes that was most successful, consequently influencing foreign impressions of Indian food. Yet, as delicious and satisfying as the standard Indian restaurant menu might be, authentic Indian cuisine offers much more.

Looking through any list of authentic Indian recipes, the one dish that won't be included is a "curry." This is because the word is simply an Anglicization of the Tamil word "*kari*," which can mean two things: the leaves of the *kari* plant or

Although many cooks still grind spices daily, traditions are starting to change

a southern Indian technique of sautéing vegetables with a masala called *kari podi*, hence the term "curry powder." By the end of the British Raj, however, the definition of the "curry" had been expanded to mean any spicy stew-like dish served with rice and the flatbreads called chapatis, and it is now often used by Westerners to describe all Indian food. Quite a mistake!

Curry powder is anathema to Indian cooks. Instead, different combinations of spices are ground into a masala to flavor specific dishes. Although many cooks still grind spices daily, traditions are starting to change as Indian food stores sell packages of prepared masalas, though never a generic curry powder.

A culinary tour of India

To appreciate the variety of authentic Indian food, it would be necessary to travel the length and breadth of the country, ideally dining in private homes. Tourists can eat well in India, but the numerous hotel buffets generally prepare dishes that have been tailored to suit Western tastes. Much of the food on offer is not much different from that available at any Indian restaurant back home.

Northern India

Rogan Josh (see page 129), Lamb Pasanda (see page 130), Tandoori Chicken (see page 156), Naans (see page 235), and other familiar Indian restaurant favorites come from northern India, which makes it an ideal starting point for a culinary tour. North India stretches from Rajasthan to Haryana, the Punjab, disputed Jammu and Kashmir along the Pakistan border, through Himachal and Uttar

Pradesh and Bihar eastward to the remote state of Arunachal Pradesh, bordering China in the northeast. It encompasses rugged mountain ranges, mighty rivers, and arid deserts.

The popular basmati and patna rices are harvested here, as are Assam and Darjeeling teas for export around the world. The Punjab is known as the "bread basket" of India for the amount of wheat it grows, supplying local needs as well as the rest of the

An elephant strides past a crowd waiting outside a Hindu temple complex

country. Nowhere else in India is meat so popular as it is in this heterogeneous region. The Punjab is the home of Sikhism, and most Sikhs eat all meats except beef. The Rajputs of Rajasthan also avoid beef, but have a long tradition as warriors and hunters, so game as well as meat is part of their culinary history. In the grass-covered Himalayan foothills of Kashmir excellent lamb is produced, which replaces goat in most local meals.

The Punjab is the home of tandoori cooking. The simple conical clay ovens, heated by glowing charcoal or wood in the bottom, are still shaped by hand and left to dry in the sun as they were 500 years ago when they were introduced by the invading Moghuls. The high temperature in the bottom heats the sides so that

16

Much of the distinctive flavor of northern cooking is from the judicious use of garam masala

food cooks quickly and remains tender on the inside. Open at the top and shaped like Ali Baba baskets, *tandoor* ovens range from 12 inches/30 cm tall to higher than an upright person. Tender marinated and spiced goat, lamb, and chicken kabobs are cooked in *tandoor* ovens and served with one of the myriad dried bean, pea, or lentil dishes (dals) and a bread everywhere in the Punjab and other parts of northern India.

Rice is an optional extra in the north of India, except in Kashmir, where it replaces bread in most meals. For the rest of the region, bread accompanies every meal, be it the flatbreads, chapatis or parathas, or leavened naans cooked on the side of a *tandoor* oven. *Roti*, the most basic flatbread, is also eaten by millions every day and is served in the large communal dining halls run by Sikh temples.

Dairy products add richness to northern cooking. Ghee, the Indian form of clarified butter, is the favored cooking fat, and yogurt is used for everything from cool, refreshing lassis to drink to tenderizing marinades for tandoori recipes. It is also curdled and pressed into paneer, the white cheese that is a prime source of protein for vegetarians. Butter is called *makhani*, lending its name to such dishes as *Murgh Makhani*, or Butter Chicken (see page 158), the popular restaurant and party dish.

Greens, such as spinach and mustard leaves, are slowly cooked to combine with dried lentils, beans, or peas, or enriched with paneer or butter. The dish *Saag Paneer* (see page 99) comes from this region.

Much of the distinctive flavor of northern cooking is from the judicious use of garam masala, a flavoring virtually unknown in the south. This traditional mix of spices is intended to warm the body from the inside.

Central India

Continuing southward, central India, made up of the predominantly vegetarian state of Gujarat on the west coast, Maharashtra, Orissa, and Andhra Pradesh slightly to the south, and fish-loving Bengal on the east coast, offers many taste sensations for the foodie traveler. The food is varied and diverse, but pan-fried seafood is enormously popular on both coasts and rice begins to replace wheat as the staple starch.

Gujarati cuisine is known first and foremost for its outstanding vegetarian food and the imaginative use of dals. Every type of dried lentil, bean, and pea is utilized, including the black chickpea (*kala chana*), which is not widely known outside India. White chickpeas are equally popular and the dried variety is finely ground into besan, or gram, flour. This creamy colored flour with a slightly earthy flavor is used to replace wheat flour in the batter for the popular potato pakoras. It's also used to make Khandvi (see page 47), the thinly rolled Italian gnocchi-like pie dough that is finished with quickly sautéed spices and seeds. This snack is particularly popular with Jains because it doesn't contain any onion or garlic.

For a rich and creamy dessert from the region that graces religious and wedding celebration tables in all parts of the country, try Shrikhand on page 207, flavored with ground cardamom and golden saffron.

Mumbai (formerly Bombay) has a long history as a trading port, so food in this capital city of Maharashtra has always absorbed outside influences,

Right *Fruits and vegetables for sale in Indian markets are always seasonal and locally grown*

Overleaf *The Gadi Sagar tank provides water for the desert city of Jaisalmer in Rajasthan*

Known as the "darling of the waters," hilsa has a life cycle similar to that of salmon

with exciting, spicy results. The city's long maritime history and large number of hotels that accommodate a constant flow of foreigners means it is like a one-stop shop to sample cooking from all of India, as well as Chinese and European fare. Traditional dishes are available, but there are also many opportunities to sample modern cooking from young chefs who want to give Indian food a lighter touch.

Mumbai's Chowpatty Beach is the ultimate destination for anyone on a culinary tour who wants to sample a wide array of Indian snacks, or *chaat*, and other street food. Despite this, Western fast-food outlets have started opening in Mumbai and all the other major cities with beef-free menus, but the endearing tradition of the daily delivery of homecooked lunches for office workers doesn't look in danger of being replaced by mass-produced sandwiches or chicken burgers. Each working day, in suburbs and rural communities all around Mumbai, tiered containers called *dabbas* are filled with complete hot, fresh meals and dispatched on a late morning train to the city. As thousands of the identical-looking *dabbas* arrive at the main railroad terminus, teams of *dabba wallas* collect and deliver them to the correct desks in offices across the city with miraculous accuracy—it is an amazing feat of organization. After lunch the process is repeated in reverse, with the empty *dabbas* arriving at the correct homes. Who in their right mind would want to swap a spiced dal, such as lentils with spinach, a vegetable dish, rice, a fresh chapati, and a selection of flavorsome chutneys and a raita for a mass-produced chicken burger?

Agriculture is the major source of income for Maharashtrians, and for more than a century Mumbai's noisy and colorful Victorian Crawford Market, renamed Jyotiba Phule Market, was the city's largest wholesale fruit and vegetable market. Produce from all of India passed through the French Gothic-style building. However, recently the market has moved out of the center in an attempt to relieve inner-city congestion. The deep-sea Koli fishermen, with their brightly colored boats, provide a steady supply of fresh seafood for broiling, pan-frying, and baking, and the highly prized butterfish comes from along the Mumbai coast. Typically, Maharashtrian food, described on Indian menus as *Marathani*, includes peanuts and cashew nuts, such as in the Lamb Shanks Marathani recipe on page 142.

Mumbai, with its Towers of Silence, is also home to India's main Parsi community, known for their deliciously spiced food. Try the Lamb Dhansak recipe on page 138 for a traditional Parsi dish that is often served with glasses of ice-cold beer. Brown rice is the usual accompaniment, but plain basmati rice is also suitable. Another typically Parsi dish is scrambled eggs given a spicy edge with chopped green chilies and cilantro: a better wake-up call than a cup of coffee in the morning.

Traveling eastward, fish is king in Bengal where the Ganges and the rivers flowing down from the Himalayas reach the Bay of Bengal. Many Bengalis consider a meal incomplete if it doesn't include fish. Hilsa, or *elish*, a member of the shad family, is the most popular species. Known as the "darling of the waters," hilsa has a life cycle similar to that of salmon: the shimmering silver-gray fish begins life in the sea, spawns in the estuary where the rivers meet the Bay of Bengal, then begins a slow journey up the

There are at least 5 million holy men in India, many of whom grow their hair long to emulate Lord Shiva

A working camel marches through a busy street in Jaipur in Rajasthan

rivers to the north of the country. It is on this northward journey, after the monsoon season, that Bengali fishermen set out at night to make their catch. The only problem with this delicacy, which can be cooked like herring, shad, or salmon, is the tremendous number of bones. Foreigners as well as Indians have to use their fingers to eat hilsa.

The annual monsoon rains, when they come, are strongest in Bengal, producing ideal conditions for farmers. In a good year, tropical fruits thrive and bananas, coconut, pineapples, and pomelos are plentiful here. The fertile soil also yields tea, coffee, corn, tapioca, cocoa, and a host of spices. The British introduced the potato, from which Anglo-Indians have created numerous recipes, and pumpkin is another favorite vegetable. Of course, coconut is abundant along the coast and finds its way into all sorts of foods, from snacks to the sweetmeats for which Kolkata is famed.

Sugar cane also thrives in the Bengali climate, so sweetness works its way into savory dishes as well as sweetmeats. Try the Sweet-and-Sour Lentils recipe on page 114 to sample this intriguing mix of sweet and savory.

Like Mumbai, Kolkata offers an amazing range of *chaat* and street foods, with hawkers pushing carts along the crowded thoroughfares. The city also has a tradition of café society, where intellectuals and academics meet to talk over cups of Masala Tea (see page 214) and a steady stream of sweetmeats.

Bengali seafood, dal, and vegetable dishes are given their regional character by being cooked with mustard oil and flavored with *panch phoron*, the masala of the region. It is made by toasting equal quantities of mustard, cumin, fennel, fenugreek, and nigella seeds, then used whole or ground into powder.

Hyderabad, in the center of Andhra Pradesh, has a long history of scholarship and is also known for its extravagant saffron-infused meat and rice biryanis, which once graced the ruling Nizams' tables. Like the Moghul rulers before them, the extraordinarily wealthy Muslim Nizams presided over lavish feasts and banquets. The city is a must-stop for anyone on a culinary tour of India. The slightly streamlined Lamb Biryani on page 126 has been adapted for modern tastes, but it is still a fragrant and flavorsome mix of basmati rice, spices—garam masala, cinnamon, cumin, chili, and turmeric—and meltingly tender lamb. Coastal food in Andhra Pradesh includes spiced fish and shrimp cooked in sesame and coconut oils, and vegetables, such as okra, flavored with fresh herbs and spices.

Southern India

Spices and seafood are two of the culinary joys of any visit to southern India and both are abundant. Sunny, palm-fringed Kerala, Karnataka, and Tamil Nadu offer the lightest food in India with spicy flavors.

Spices are not only a flavoring in south India. Spice growing is big business and peppercorns were once known as "black gold." Kochi (formerly Cochin) is the center of India's spice trade, and the aromas of cardamom, coriander, cumin, cinnamon, and vanilla wafting out of warehouses scent the air in the old town with its winding narrow streets and antique stores. Any visit to southern India should

Spices and seafood are two of the culinary joys of any visit to southern India and both are abundant

include a stop at a spice plantation to view favorite flavorings growing in their natural habitat and taste them at their freshest.

The pale green cardamoms, red and green chilies, curry leaves, mustard seeds, and golden turmeric used in southern Indian cooking give the food a vibrant appearance as well as flavor. Many traditional dishes also have a distinctive sharp, sour taste derived from tamarind pulp.

Fresh coconut plantations stretch as far as the eyes can see in this part of India, and coconut trees also grow easily in domestic gardens in this tropical climate, so coconut is also a popular, everyday flavoring that finds its way into dishes from snacks through desserts. Boat tours along Kerala's waterways can also include a stop at a coconut plantation to sample just-off-the-tree coconut flesh and milk: much milder than when coconuts have aged during travel to Western supermarkets.

Rice is the predominant starch in the south and the natural partner to serve with the soup-like dals, such as Sambhar (see page 82), which is eaten by millions every day. Rice is also used to make the crêpes and steamed rice cakes that are unique to the region: fermented rice and black lentils are ground into a batter for thin, crisp Dosas (see page 243), and steamed flying-saucer-looking *idlis* are served for breakfasts, often with a highly spiced dal that starts the day with a kick. *Upama*, a steamed semolina cake flavored with curry leaves, mustard leaves, and chili, is another rice cake eaten at breakfast or as a snack.

Kerala, with its harmonious mix of Hindus, Muslims, Christians, and a Jewish community in Kochi, has an

24

Enjoying an Indian meal in India is very different from dining in Western Indian restaurants

interesting cuisine. An impressive variety of fish and shellfish, from the Arabian Sea as well as the intercoastal network of waterways, is always available, but dals and even beef are served here. For seafood with a just-caught flavor, try one of the ramshackle eating huts across from the Chinese fishing nets along the harbor at Fort Kochi.

The hot, chili-spiced food characteristically prepared around Chennai (formerly Madras) is now mistakenly taken to represent all Indian cooking to people who prefer milder food. The liberal use of chilies, however, is designed to counter the tropical heat. As the chilies warm the body from the inside, perspiration cools the body on the outside. The Beef Madras recipe on page 152 showcases the popular flavor combination of chilies and coconut.

Cashew nuts flourish in the long, dry growing season in Karnataka, as well as in Goa and Kerala, so anyone who enjoys them only in small amounts elsewhere, because of the cost, can really indulge here. Bowls are constantly refilled in hotel bars. In March, visit the markets to see the freshly harvested nuts still attached to the green fruits.

At the southern tip of Tamil Nadu the numerous temple cities offer some of India's most fascinating architecture and outstanding vegetarian food, based on spicy dal stews, rice, and fresh-tasting chutneys. Coffee, a cash crop, is also drunk throughout the day here, much like spiced tea in other parts of India.

Eating the Indian way

Enjoying an Indian meal in India is very different from dining in Western Indian restaurants, even if the dishes are identical. The concept of serving a series of courses is alien to most Indians. Instead, the entire meal, including dessert, is presented at once. The traditional method for this is to serve the different dishes in small bowls called *katoris* on a round metal plate called a *thali,* which can be as utilitarian as stainless steel, as elaborate as decorated gold or silver, or, in the south, as charming as a large banana leaf. As styles change, however, this is becoming more a method of restaurant presentation than one used for family meals. Today home meals are just as likely to be served Western "family style," with all the dishes in the center of the table for everyone to help themselves.

When an Indian cook plans a *thali* meal, he or she first decides the main dish, be it chicken, meat, or a dal. Next, a vegetable dish with complementary flavors and a raita will be decided on, then the type of rice and/or bread and chutneys will be selected. As with a Western meal, the cook strives for a combination of textures and flavors as well as colors. A "veg" *thali,* for example, might consist of a dal, with two or three vegetable dishes, such as Okra Bhaji (see page 106), Matar Paneer (see page 100), and Raita Potatoes (see page 52), along with one or two chutneys, arranged around a mound of rice in the center. A chapati might be added as well.

The Indian skill of eating with the fingers takes great practice. All Indians agree that only the right hand is used, but that is where the consensus ends. Northerners use only the very tips of their fingers to tear a piece of bread to scoop up bite-size portions of food, then watch in horror as southerners use their fingers to scoop up their food.

A woman sells fresh fruit on Goa's popular Benaulim Beach

In the Indian kitchen

It has never been easier for non-Indian cooks to capture the diverse and fragrant flavors of Indian food. Ingredients can now be found in Asian and Indian food stores as well as in some supermarkets.

Banana leaves Southern Indian food served on these large, glossy, dark green leaves looks as stunning as it tastes. The leaves can also be wrapped around food before cooking. The leaves are sold fresh in Indian and other Asian food stores.

Basmati rice (basmati chaaval) Grown in the foothills of the Himalayas, this is the long-grain rice used in the recipes in this book. It is valued around the world for its delicate fragrance and silky grains that remain separate during cooking. Outside of India, basmati rice is synonymous with Indian food, but more than 20 varieties of rice are grown and used within the country. Consequently, basmati is often saved for special occasions and celebrations. This is the rice to use for lavish biryanis and pilafs.

Basmati rice traditionally requires extensive rinsing and soaking before cooking, but some supermarket brands recommend skipping this step. Always read the package before cooking.

To prepare perfect basmati rice, rinse a scant ⅓ cup per person under cold water until the water runs clear. Put the rice in a bowl with water to cover and let soak for 30 minutes. Drain the rice and put in a heavy-bottom pan with a tight-fitting lid. Add enough water to cover (the exact amount does not matter) and a large pinch of salt and bring to a boil, then boil, uncovered, for 6 minutes. Drain in a strainer or colander that will fit in the pan, but do not rinse. Put a shallow layer of water in the bottom of the pan and put the strainer or colander on top, without letting the rice touch the water. Cover with

the lid and steam over medium heat for about 4 minutes. Fluff with a fork and serve, stirring in extra salt if necessary.

Cilantro (hara dhaniya) Cilantro leaves are to Indian cooks what parsley is to Western cooks. They add a bright green colorful garnish to many dishes and a sharp flavor to breads, rice, chutneys, salads, and many drinks. The roots can also be finely chopped and added to other ingredients.

Coconut (nariyal) Considered the "fruit of the gods," coconuts are important in Hindu religious ceremonies, as well as to the kitchens of southern India and Goa. The creamy white flesh and thin, cloudy coconut water are used in cooking and as snacks. Coconut cream and the thinner coconut milk are available in cans or can be made by soaking freshly grated coconut flesh in boiling water. If using canned coconut cream, be sure to buy the unsweetened variety.

The quickest way to add a rich coconut flavor to curries without the fuss of opening a fresh coconut is to dissolve a specified amount of creamed coconut in boiling water. Pressed bars of white creamed coconut are available.

Curry leaves (kadhi patta) These thin, pointed green leaves, which look like miniature bay leaves, grow on trees native to India and Sri Lanka. They are so called because the whole tree gives off a "curry" aroma. The leaves are often sautéed and added at the end of cooking for a garnish, giving an aromatic, slightly bitter flavor to primarily southern Indian dishes. Buy fresh or dried.

Fenugreek (methi) Small, irregular-shaped fenugreek seeds are one of the flavorings included in commercial curry powders, but they are less used in Indian masalas. Fenugreek seeds are added to dals to help counter flatulence. The seeds are often sautéed at the beginning of a recipe, but take care because they taste bitter if overcooked. Fresh fenugreek leaves can be cooked like spinach. Ground fenugreek and fenugreek seeds are sold at supermarkets. Fresh and dried leaves are available from Indian food stores.

Ginger (adrak) Anyone who wants to add an authentic flavor to their Indian cooking should stock up on this knobbly rhizome. The warm, spicy taste is essential to so many meat, poultry, and fish dishes, as well as numerous vegetarian favorites. For the best flavor, buy fresh ginger with a tight, smooth skin. A wrinkled skin is an indication that the flesh is drying out. Store in a covered container in the refrigerator. Ginger is often ground into a paste before cooking, and many of the recipes in this book start with sautéing a paste made from ginger and garlic.

To make the **Garlic and Ginger Paste**, blend together equal quantities of garlic and ginger. Because the quantities required are often too small to process in a food processor or blender, it is a good idea to make a larger quantity and store it in a sealed jar in the refrigerator for up to three weeks, or in the freezer for up to one month. Alternatively, you can grind the required amount for a specific recipe using a spice grinder or pestle and mortar.

Jaggery (gur) A by-product in the production of sugar from sugar cane, this sweetener is used in place of sugar in many Indian recipes, especially candy. It is sold in a cone or barrel shape in Indian food stores. Brown or raw sugar can be used instead.

Mint (pudina) Introduced to India by the Persians, this fresh-tasting herb is particularly popular in

northern India, where it garnishes rich meat and poultry dishes. Fresh mint also flavors many chutneys, raitas, and drinks.

Mustard oil (sarson ka tel) A popular cooking oil with a strong, pungent flavor. To counter the pronounced flavor, many recipes begin by heating the oil until it is very hot and then letting it cool before reheating and adding other ingredients. Look for this in Indian food stores and some supermarkets.

Silver foil (varak) Indian desserts and candy are elevated to special status with a decoration of edible silver dust pressed into ultra-thin sheets more delicate than foil. Easy to use, this shimmering decoration is sold in Indian food stores.

Tamarind (imli) When an Indian dish has a distinctive and pronounced sour flavor, such as Sweet-and-Sour Lentils (see page 114), there is a good chance it includes one form or another of this pulp taken from tamarind pods. Supermarkets sell pots of ready-to-use tamarind paste or you can buy tamarind as a compressed slab that needs to be reconstituted with boiling water, then strained.

Yogurt (dahi) There are countless uses for plain yogurt in the Indian kitchen. It is used as a tenderizer and a souring agent, as well as the main ingredient in numerous raitas and some chutneys. Yogurt, referred to as "curd" in Indian recipes, is made from buffalo milk and served in one form or another at most Indian meals. The cool and refreshing Salt Lassi (see page 212) is made with yogurt, and in some regions every meal ends with a bowl of yogurt. For a special indulgent dessert, try Shrikhand (see page 207), strained yogurt delicately flavored with cardamom and saffron.

In the Indian spice box

Indian food without spices is like a garden without flowers. Spices are the essence of Indian cooking. A walk through any Indian spice market assaults the senses on two fronts: the heady aroma is exotic and tantalizing, and the kaleidoscope of colors is dazzling. Mounds of vibrant red ground chilies, golden tamarind, pale green cardamom pods, jet-black nigella seeds, gray poppy seeds, and creamy sesame spilling out of burlap sacks can give the visit an almost magical feel.

Curry powder as such is not used in India. Instead, Indian cooks skillfully combine spices to give each dish its own character with a distinctive flavor and color. Prepared spice mixtures called masalas are sold in India just as they are in the West, but the tradition of combining and grinding spices for each meal is still widely practiced.

Below are the spices that contribute an authentic flavor to the recipes in this book. Ready-ground spices are convenient, but they lose their flavor more quickly than whole spices that are ground as they are required.

Asafoetida (hing) It's not for nothing that this finely ground resin is known as "the devil's dung," because the pungent sulphurous aroma is very off-putting until it is cooked. Indian cooks include asafoetida in vegetables, dals, pickles, and other dishes for its digestive qualities, and Hindu Brahmins and Jains use it to replace the flavor of forbidden garlic and onion. Asafoetida is used only in small amounts and it is sold in small, airtight containers in Indian food stores.

Cardamom (elaichi) Known as the "queen of spices" (black pepper is the "king"), green cardamom is one of the most popular flavorings in Indian cooking, used in both savory and sweet dishes as well as drinks. The delicate, sweet aroma comes from the tiny seeds contained in the small, smooth pods. Even though the whole pods are often included in dishes, they are not meant to be eaten, although chewing cardamom pods as a breath freshener dates from Moghul times. Black cardamom has a much heavier, pronounced flavor and is only used in savory recipes. Cardamom is widely available in supermarkets, ground or in pods, which retain their freshness for longer.

Chilies, green and red (hari mirch and lal mirch) Synonymous as chilies are with Indian food, they are relative newcomers to the Indian spice box, having been introduced by the Portuguese. More than 20 varieties of chilies grow in India now, with colors ranging from white and saffron yellow to the more familiar red and green ones. Green chilies are unripe red chilies.

Unfortunately, it is difficult to tell how hot a chili is by appearance only. As a general rule, the smaller and redder a chili, the hotter it will be, although experience is a better guide. The amount of heat any particular chili adds to a dish depends on whether or not it is seeded. The more seeds left in, the hotter the dish will be. Dried red chilies have a very concentrated flavor and therefore should be used only in small amounts.

Chili powder Kashmiri chilies are the dark red chilies that grow in the northern region of Kashmir. They are mild tasting and are valued for the vibrant red color they add to dishes such as Rogan Josh (see page 129) and Tandoori Chicken (see page 156), rather than for their flavor. Look for this chili powder in Indian food stores. Cayenne chili powder, available in all supermarkets, is the variety to use for heat rather than color.

Cinnamon (dalchini) As in other countries, Indian cooks use this ground spice or the rolled, thin quills of the cinnamon tree bark to flavor sweet and savory dishes and drinks. Cinnamon is one of the essential spices in Garam Masala (see page 251), used to flavor so many northern curries and rice dishes. Toasting cinnamon in a dry pan before adding it to other ingredients helps to intensify its flavor.

Cloves (laung) More frequently used whole than ground in Indian cooking, these dried flowerbuds have a strong aromatic flavor that can be overpowering if used in abundance or chewed. Cloves feature in northern Indian savory and sweet recipes, and are used in *paan*, the mix of spices and leaves that is sold on many street corners as a mouth freshener.

Coriander (dhaniya) One of the unmistakable savory flavors of Indian food is ground roasted coriander seeds. The seeds, which taste very different from the vibrant green leaves of the fresh herb, cilantro, are round with very thin ridges and easily ground in a spice blender or using a pestle and mortar. They are sold as seeds or a ground powder.

Cumin (jeera) Popular with cooks in all regions of India, cumin is prized for its distinctive, strong flavor and digestive qualities. Many recipes start with sautéing the thin, slightly elongated seeds in hot oil to intensify the flavor and help spread it throughout the dish, but watch closely as they can burn and become bitter tasting in a matter of seconds. Brown cumin seeds, familiar to cooks throughout the West, are readily available, but black cumin seeds (*kala jeera*) are found in Indian food stores.

Ground mango (amchoor powder) A powder made from green mangoes and used as a meat tenderizer, in sour dishes, or in chaat masala. It is available in Indian food stores.

Mustard seeds (rai) Tiny round black, brown, and yellow mustard seeds are used throughout India. They are hot and spicy when raw, but are often sautéed in hot oil until they jump to temper their flavor. Black and brown mustard seeds can be used interchangeably. They are sold in supermarkets.

Nigella seeds (kalonji) Also known as black onion seeds (although they have nothing to do with onions), these small dark-black seeds look like tiny chips of coal and are added to fish, pickles, naans, rice, and dried bean, pea, and lentil dishes. Their flavor is nutty and peppery.

Saffron (kesar) The most expensive spice in the world, these thin threads come from the dried stamens of the crocus flower and are so costly because the stamens are hand-picked. Indian saffron is grown in Kashmir and used to add a brilliant golden color and a distinctive, slightly musky taste to many Indian dishes, mostly those from the north. Used since Moghul times, saffron is rarely missing from such classic dishes as Lamb Biryani (see page 126) and special desserts. Indian "saffron" that seems reasonably priced is more likely actually to be safflower, which, although it adds an orange-yellow tint to other ingredients, doesn't have any flavor.

Turmeric (haldi) The instant sunshine of many Indian dishes. Turmeric, a member of the ginger family, adds a golden yellow color and a pungent flavor to meat, seafood, vegetable, and dried bean, pea, and lentil dishes. The ground version is sold in supermarkets, but for the fresh or dry rhizomes go to a large Indian food store.

SNACKS &
APPETIZERS

32 Street food is popular throughout Asia, but nowhere more so than in India. Eating on the go from dawn to dusk is part of daily life for many Indians. Wherever people congregate, especially in the overcrowded cities and in markets or bazaars, at busy intersections, outside stores, at railroad and bus stations and taxi stands, there will be at least one person selling bags of snack mixes called *bhujiyas* (known outside India generically as Bombay mix) or squatting over makeshift heat sources cooking kabobs, pakoras, or samosas, or pushing fruits through a juicer for fresh drinks.

The snack sellers' cries, the sizzling hot oil, and the mixed scents of spices and dust are all part of the backdrop to so many Indian experiences.

Small, savory Indian snacks are called *chaat*, which comes from the Hindi word meaning "to lick." This is because *chaat* are considered "finger-licking good." They can be enjoyed hot or cold, and are chili hot and spicy to taste. *Chaat* are inexpensive, varied, and usually a mix of tantalizing flavors. In other words, they are perfect for munching while walking along and chatting with friends.

Of course, it is easy to over-romanticize Indian street food, but much of it is good and satisfying, and the choices are endless. The ingenious, resourceful army of India's street cooks take the place of Western fast-food outlets, which are still few and far between in Indian cities and nonexistent in rural areas. The exciting, varied tradition of Indian street food also survives because in many overcrowded city dwellings kitchen space is limited, if it exists at all.

For many, Indian snack and street-food culture reaches its height at Mumbai's Chowpatty Beach. In a city as densely populated as Mumbai, the beach's open space and amusement rides with their bright garish lights serve as a magnet for fast-food cooks and hungry patrons alike as the sun begins to set. Bhel Poori (see page 44), a jumbled mix of spiced diced potatoes, puffed rice, and ultra-thin sev noodles, tempered with a mixture of sour tamarind chutney, spicy and refreshing cilantro chutney, and a dollop of yogurt, is often cited as the best example of a uniquely Indian *chaat*. Each of the open-air vendors offers a unique recipe, but whichever one is sampled it will be an unmistakable taste of Mumbai. On hot, steamy nights, courting couples and families with young children relax and cool off with a creamy Indian ice cream called Kulfi, such as the version flavored with saffron and almonds on page 204.

And to drink with *chaat*? Masala Tea (see page 214) is a natural choice as Indians seem to drink it all day long, but a Salt Lassi (see page 212) and Mango Lassi (see page 213) are also popular. Or open an ice-cold

Small, savory Indian snacks are called chaat, *which comes from the Hindi word meaning "to lick"*

34

Soups are not a traditional part of Indian meals, but were introduced by the British during the Raj

bottle of one of the Indian beers that are now available around the world.

Serving a separate first course is not a traditional part of Indian family meals, so it is with a certain amount of latitude that Indian restaurant menus outside the country feature the most popular Indian *chaat* and other street food as "appetizers". Onion Bhaji (see page 38), Golden Cauliflower Pakoras (see page 42), Vegetarian Samosas (see page 40), and Chicken Tikka (see page 55) are all examples of popular Indian street food.

Soups are also not a traditional part of Indian meals, but were introduced by the British during the Raj. Memsahib's Mulligatawny Soup (see page 68), for example, is a legacy of British rule. Missing the soups from home, British cooks took Rasam (see page 71), a spicy Tamil broth, added mutton to make it more substantial, and called the result "Mulligatawny," which loosely translates as "pepper water." Try both recipes to appreciate the similarities and differences.

Most of the recipes in this chapter illustrate the versatility of Indian snacks. Munch these dishes as snacks throughout the day, or serve them before a more substantial entrée or with chilled cocktails before dinner. For snack ideas from other chapters, try Dosa Masala (see page 84), Parsi Scrambled Eggs (see page 89), and Fish Pakoras (see page 190).

Detail of a door arch in Jaipur's City Palace, which is famous for its elaborate art and architecture

Overleaf *The beautiful Pushkar Lake in Rajasthan is overlooked by grand buildings*

38 onion bhaji
pyaaz pakora

There can't be many Indian restaurants, in India or elsewhere, that don't feature this popular snack, or chaat, *on the menu. Wherever you are in India, you'll find street vendors cooking bhajis and other snacks in large, black, wok-like vessels called kadhais. In your kitchen, however, a large, heavy-bottom pan, wok, or deep-fat fryer will do the job just as efficiently.*

MAKES 12

1 cup besan or gram flour

1 tsp salt

1 tsp ground cumin

1 tsp ground turmeric

1 tsp baking soda

1/2 tsp chili powder

2 tsp lemon juice

2 tbsp vegetable or peanut oil, plus
  extra for deep-frying

2–8 tbsp water

2 onions, thinly sliced

2 tsp coriander seeds, lightly crushed

lemon wedges, to serve

1 Sift the besan flour, salt, cumin, turmeric, baking soda, and chili powder into a large bowl. Add the lemon juice and the oil, then very gradually stir in just enough water until a batter similar to light cream forms. Mix in the onions and coriander seeds.

2 Heat enough oil for deep-frying* in a kadhai, wok, deep-fat fryer, or large, heavy-bottom pan until it reaches 350°F/180°C, or until a cube of bread browns in 30 seconds. Without overcrowding the pan, drop in §spoonfuls of the onion mixture and cook for 2 minutes, then use tongs to flip the bhajis over and cook for an additional 2 minutes, or until golden brown.

3 Immediately remove the bhajis from the oil and drain well on crumpled paper towels. Keep the bhajis warm while you continue cooking the remaining batter. Serve hot with lemon wedges.

*cook's tip
As with all deep-fried food, the fine line between light crispiness and greasiness depends on keeping the oil at the correct temperature while the bhajis are cooking. If it is too low, the bhajis will be greasy; too hot, and the coating will burn while the onions remain raw. This is why you should cook the bhajis in batches and let the oil return to the correct temperature between batches. If you do lots of deep-fat frying, it is worth investing in a thermometer.

40 vegetarian samosas
aloo mattar samosa

It takes a little practice and patience to get the hang of shaping these triangular-shaped pastries, but after you've rolled out and filled a couple, you will become as proficient as India's seemingly endless army of street cooks. "Veg" or "non-veg" samosas are cooked and sold at every street market and busy intersection.

MAKES 14

1³/₄ cups all-purpose flour

¹/₂ tsp salt

3 tbsp Ghee (see page 253) or butter, melted

¹/₂ tbsp lemon juice

¹/₃–¹/₂ cup cold water

for the filling*

4 tbsp Ghee (see page 253) or vegetable or peanut oil

1 onion, very finely chopped

2 garlic cloves, crushed

1 potato, very finely diced

2 carrots, very finely chopped

2 tsp mild, medium, or hot curry powder, to taste

1¹/₂ tsp ground coriander

1 tsp ground turmeric

1 fresh green chili, seeded and finely chopped

1 tsp salt

¹/₂ tsp black mustard seeds

1¹/₄ cups water

scant 1 cup frozen peas

2 oz/55 g cauliflower florets, broken into the smallest florets possible

vegetable or peanut oil, for frying

fresh cilantro leaves, to garnish

1 To make the filling, melt the ghee in a kadhai, wok, or large skillet over medium-high heat. Add the onion and garlic and sauté for 5–8 minutes until soft but not brown.

2 Stir in the potato and carrots and continue sautéing, stirring occasionally, for 5 minutes. Stir in the curry powder, coriander, turmeric, chili, salt, and mustard seeds. Pour in the water and bring to a boil. Reduce the heat to very low and simmer, uncovered, for about 15 minutes, stirring occasionally. Add the peas and cauliflower florets and continue simmering until all the vegetables are tender and the liquid evaporates. Remove from the heat and set aside.

3 Meanwhile, to make the pie dough, sift the flour and salt into a bowl. Make a well in the center, add the ghee and lemon juice, and work them into the flour with your fingertips. Gradually add the water until the mixture comes together to form a soft dough.

4 Tip the dough on to the counter and knead for about 10 minutes until smooth. Shape into a ball, cover with a damp dish towel, and let rest for about 15 minutes.

5 To shape the dough, divide into 7 equal pieces. Work with 1 piece at a time and keep the pieces you aren't working with covered with a dish towel. Roll the piece you are working with into an 8-inch/20-cm circle on a lightly greased counter, then cut in half to make 2 equal semicircles. Continue to cut out ·12 more semicircles.

6 Working with one semicircle at a time, wet the edges with water. Place about 2 teaspoons of the filling on the dough, just off center. Fold one side into

the center, covering the filling. Fold the other side in the opposite direction, overlapping the first fold to form a cone shape. Wet the open edge with more water and press down to seal. Cover with a damp dish towel while you continue to assemble the remaining samosas.

7 Heat about 1 inch/2.5 cm of oil in a kadhai, wok, or large, heavy-bottom pan until it reaches 350°F/180°C, or until a cube of bread browns in 30 seconds. Cook the samosas in batches for 2–3 minutes, flipping them over once, until golden brown, then drain well on crumpled paper towels. These are best served warm with cilantro leaves to garnish and a chutney, but are also good eaten at room temperature.

*cook's tip
If you prefer "non-veg" samosas, use the Kheema Matar (see page 151) recipe as a filling, simmering the mixture in an uncovered pan until it is dry.

42

golden cauliflower pakoras
gobhi ka pakora

These golden, crisp fritters appear on restaurant menus in the West, while in India they are more likely to be prepared in homes as part of a meal or as a snack, rather than being cooked on the street.

SERVES 4

vegetable or peanut oil, for deep-frying

14 oz/400 g cauliflower florets

for the batter

1 cup besan or gram flour

2 tsp ground coriander

1 tsp Garam Masala (see page 251)

1 tsp salt

$^1\!/_2$ tsp ground turmeric

pinch of chili powder

1 tbsp Ghee (see page 253), melted, or vegetable
  or peanut oil

1 tsp lemon juice

$^2\!/_3$ cup cold water

2 tsp nigella seeds

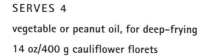

1 To make the batter*, stir the besan flour, coriander, garam masala, salt, turmeric, and chili powder into a large bowl. Make a well in the center, add the ghee and lemon juice with 2 tablespoons of the water and stir together to make a thick batter.

2 Slowly beat in enough of the remaining water with an electric hand-held mixer or a whisk to make a smooth batter about the same thickness as heavy cream. Stir in the nigella seeds. Cover the bowl and let stand for at least 30 minutes.

3 When you are ready to cook, heat enough oil for deep-frying in a kadhai, wok, deep-fat fryer, or large, heavy-bottom pan until it reaches 350°F/180°C, or until a cube of bread browns in 30 seconds. Dip one cauliflower floret at a time into the batter and let any excess batter fall back into the bowl, then drop it into the hot oil. Add a few more dipped florets, without overcrowding the pan, and cook for about 3 minutes, or until golden brown and crisp.

4 Use a slotted spoon to remove the fritters from the oil and drain well on crumpled paper towels. Continue cooking until all the cauliflower florets and batter have been used. Serve the hot fritters with a chutney for dipping.

*cook's tip
You can make the batter a day ahead and refrigerate overnight, but let it return to room temperature and beat it well before you use it.

sweet and spicy nuts 43
khatta-meetha mewa

After a long day's sightseeing in the pulsating heat of Mumbai, a hotel's cocktail lounge can be a tranquil refuge and you will almost certainly be served a bowl of cashew nuts or almonds to nibble on with a cooling drink. Enjoy this spicy combination with an ice-cold beer or Salt Lassi (see page 212).

MAKES 3 CUPS

1¹/₂ **cups superfine sugar**

1 **tsp sea salt**

2 **tbsp mild, medium, or hot curry powder, to taste**

1 **tsp ground turmeric**

1 **tsp ground coriander**

pinch of chili powder

3 **cups mixed whole blanched almonds**
  and shelled cashew nuts*

vegetable or peanut oil, for deep-frying

1 Mix the sugar, salt, curry powder, turmeric, coriander, and chili powder together in a large bowl, then set aside.

2 Meanwhile, bring a large pan of water to a boil. Add the almonds and cashews and blanch for 1 minute, then tip them into a strainer to drain and shake off as much of the excess water as possible. Immediately toss the nuts with the sugar and spices.

3 Heat enough oil for deep-frying in a kadhai, wok, deep-fat fryer, or large, heavy-bottom pan to 350°F/180°C, or until a cube of bread browns in 30 seconds. Use a slotted spoon to remove the nuts from the spice mixture, leaving the spicy mixture behind in the bowl, then drop the nuts into the hot oil.

Cook them for 3–4 minutes, stirring occasionally and watching carefully because they can burn quickly, until they turn golden.

4 Remove the nuts from the oil with the slotted spoon and toss them in the remaining spice mixture. Tip the nuts into a strainer and shake off the excess spices, then let cool completely and crisp up. Store in an airtight container for up to a week.

*cook's tip
Although pecans and walnuts are not often served in India, they also taste good prepared with this spicy mixture.

44

bhel poori
bhel puri

*In Mumbai, this is a popular street chaat, unbeatable
for munching on hot, steamy nights walking along
Chowpatty Beach. No two vendors are likely to
prepare identical mixtures, but whichever one you
buy, it will include puffed rice and potatoes. The
quantities here are a suggestion and can easily be
increased or decreased to suit your personal taste.*

SERVES 4–6

salt

10¹/₂ oz/300 g new potatoes

7 oz/200 g canned chickpeas, rinsed and very
  well drained

3¹/₂ oz/100 g sev noodles*

2 oz/55 g puffed rice

4 tbsp raisins

2 tbsp chopped fresh cilantro

1 tbsp fennel seeds, toasted and cooled

12 mini Pooris (see page 240), crushed

4 tbsp plain yogurt

Tamarind Chutney (see page 249)

Cilantro Chutney (see page 245)

for the chaat masala

1 tbsp coriander seeds

1 tbsp cumin seeds

1 tsp black peppercorns

2 dried red chilies

1 Bring a large pan of salted water to a boil and cook
the potatoes for 12–15 minutes until tender. Drain
and run under cold water to cool, then peel and cut into
¹/₄-inch/5-mm dice. Cover and let chill for at least
30 minutes.

2 Meanwhile, to make the chaat masala, heat a dry
skillet over high heat. Add the coriander and cumin
seeds, peppercorns, and chilies and stir around until
they give off their aroma. Immediately tip them out of
the pan to stop the cooking, watching closely because
the cumin seeds burn quickly. Grind the toasted spice
mixture in a spice grinder or with a pestle and mortar.

3 Use your hands to toss together the potatoes,
chickpeas, sev noodles, puffed rice, raisins, cilantro,
fennel seeds, and crushed mini pooris. Sprinkle with the
chaat masala and toss again.

4 Divide the mixture among small serving bowls or
place in one large bowl and drizzle with the yogurt
and chutneys to taste. It is best eaten straight away
so it doesn't become soggy.

*cook's tip

For an authentic taste and texture, look for bags
of sev noodles in Indian food stores. They are small
pieces of extra-thin noodles, often included in
Bombay Mix recipes.

khandvi
khandvi

Served at weddings and various religious festivals, these thin, delicate besan flour rolls make an appetizing canapé with cocktails or dry white wine.

MAKES 16 ROLLS

scant ²/₃ cup besan or gram flour

1 tsp ground ginger

1 tsp salt

¹/₂ tsp ground turmeric

¹/₄ tsp chili powder, or to taste

2 cups water

³/₄ cup plain yogurt

1 tbsp lemon juice

for the garnish

2 tbsp vegetable or peanut oil

¹/₂ tbsp black mustard seeds

¹/₂ tbsp sesame seeds, toasted

1 fresh green chili, seeded and finely
  chopped (optional)

¹/₂ tbsp finely chopped fresh cilantro

1 Sift the besan flour, ginger, salt, turmeric, and chili powder together into a bowl and make a well in the center. Whisk the water, yogurt, and lemon juice together, then pour into the well in the dry ingredients and whisk until a smooth batter forms.

2 Rinse the widest and deepest pan you have with cold water, then pour in the batter. Place over high heat and bring to a boil, stirring constantly. Reduce the heat and continue simmering and stirring for about 30 minutes, or until the liquid evaporates and the mixture is thick.

3 Meanwhile, lightly grease a shallow, square 12-inch/30-cm cookie sheet*. Pour the mixture on to the cookie sheet and use a wet spatula to spread it out about ¹/₈ inch/3 mm thick. Set aside and let cool completely.

4 Use a sharp knife to cut the mixture into 8 strips, each 1¹/₂ inches/4 cm wide, then cut each strip in half so it is 6 inches/15 cm long. Use a round-bladed knife to lift up the strips, then roll them up like a jelly roll. Transfer the rolls to a serving platter and chill until required.

5 Just before serving, heat the oil in a pan or skillet over medium heat. Add the mustard and sesame seeds and cook, stirring constantly, until they start to pop. Immediately remove the pan from the heat, add the chili, and stir it around in the residual heat for 30 seconds longer, then pour the oil and spices over the rolls. Sprinkle with the cilantro and serve.

*cook's tip

If you don't have a square 12-inch/30-cm cookie sheet, simply grease the area of those measurements on a clean counter and spread the mixture out until it is ¹/₈ inch/3 mm thick.

spicy shrimp with cucumber
masala jhinga aur kakdi

48

High-tech computer industries have clustered in Bangalore, giving this ancient and traditional town a real twenty-first century feel. Along with the wealth have come new-style restaurants with young chefs giving a twist to traditional recipes, such as this dry, crunchy version of Shrimp Pooris (for a traditional recipe, see page 185).

SERVES 4–6

2 tomatoes

¼ tsp ground coriander

¼ tsp ground cumin

¼ tsp Garam Masala (see page 251)

1 onion, very finely chopped

7 oz/200 g cucumber, seeded and finely diced*

9 oz/250 g small cooked shelled shrimp, thawed if frozen

3 tbsp finely chopped fresh cilantro

salt

to serve

6–8 Pooris (see page 240)

lemon wedges

1 Bring a pan of water to a boil. Cut a small cross in the top of each tomato, then drop it in the boiling water for about 1 minute. Remove the tomatoes from the hot water and immediately plunge into ice-cold water. Peel the tomatoes, then cut them in half, scoop out the seeds, and very finely dice the flesh.

2 Put the coriander, cumin, and garam masala in a dry skillet over medium-high heat and stir for 15 seconds. Add the onion and continue stirring constantly for 2 minutes: the mixture will be very dry.

3 Add the tomatoes and cucumber to the pan and stir for 2 minutes. Add the shrimp and stir for an additional 2 minutes just to warm them through. Stir in the cilantro and salt to taste.

4 Serve hot or at room temperature with the pooris and lemon wedges for squeezing over.

*cook's tip
For a colorful, refreshing version to be served chilled, replace the cucumber with finely diced mango.

This beautifully decorative architectural style is typical of India's many grand palaces and temples

shrimp and pineapple tikka
jhinga aur annanas tikka

Not long ago, Kerala was a sleepy southern Indian backwater, but now it's a hot tourist destination. Along with its changed status have come boutique hotels, where young chefs make their mark with new-wave flavor combinations, such as this stylish appetizer. For parties, this looks attractive served on glossy banana leaves.

MAKES 4

1 tsp cumin seeds

1 tsp coriander seeds

¹/₂ tsp fennel seeds

¹/₂ tsp yellow mustard seeds

¹/₄ tsp fenugreek seeds

¹/₄ tsp nigella seeds

pinch of chili powder

salt

2 tbsp lemon or pineapple juice

12 raw jumbo shrimp, shelled, deveined, and
   tails left intact*

12 bite-size wedges of fresh or well-drained
   canned pineapple

chopped fresh cilantro, to garnish

Coconut Sambal (see page 247), to serve

1 If you are using long, wooden skewers for this rather than metal ones, place 4 skewers upright in a tall glass of water to soak for 20 minutes so they do not burn under the broiler.

2 Dry-roast the cumin, coriander, fennel, mustard, fenugreek, and nigella seeds in a hot skillet over high heat, stirring them around constantly, until you can smell the aroma of the spices. Immediately tip the spices out of the pan so they do not burn.

3 Put the spices in a spice grinder or mortar, add the chili powder and salt to taste, and grind to a fine powder. Transfer to a nonmetallic bowl and stir in the lemon or pineapple juice.

4 Add the shrimp to the bowl and stir them around so they are well coated, then set aside to marinate for 10 minutes. Meanwhile, preheat the broiler to high.

5 Thread 3 shrimp and 3 pineapple wedges alternately on to each wooden or metal skewer. Broil about 4 inches/10 cm from the heat for 2 minutes on each side, brushing with any leftover marinade, until the shrimp turn pink and are cooked through.

6 Serve the shrimp and pineapple wedges off the skewers on a plate with plenty of cilantro sprinkled over. Serve the coconut sambal on the side.

*cook's tip

To devein the shrimp, remove the shell, hold back-side up, and use a small, sharp knife to make a slash along the length of the shrimp from the back to the front, only cutting halfway through the flesh. Use the point of the knife to pick out the thin, black intestine, and discard.

52

raita potatoes
aloo ka raita

Raitas are often served as a cool, creamy accompaniment to hot, spicy Indian meals, but this potato and yogurt mixture also doubles as a flavorsome salad when served on its own. To make this more substantial for a light lunch, team the creamy mixture with rice and chapatis.

SERVES 4–6
14 oz/400 g new potatoes, scrubbed

salt

1 tsp coriander seeds

1 tsp fennel seeds

1³/₄ cups plain yogurt

1 fresh green chili, seeded and finely chopped

pepper

chopped fresh mint, to garnish

4–8 poppadoms, warmed, to serve*

1 Boil the potatoes in salted water for 10–12 minutes until tender when pierced with a fork. Drain and rinse with cold water to cool, then shake dry. When cool enough to handle, finely chop the potatoes with or without peeling them.

2 Meanwhile, dry-roast the coriander and fennel seeds in a hot skillet over high heat, stirring them around constantly, until you can smell the aromas. Immediately tip the spices out of the pan so they do not burn.

3 Put the spices in a spice grinder, or use a pestle and mortar, and grind to a fine powder.

4 Beat the yogurt in a bowl until it is smooth, then stir in the ground spices, chili, and salt and pepper to taste. Add the potato chunks and stir together without breaking up the potatoes. Cover the bowl with plastic wrap and chill for at least 30 minutes.

5 When ready to serve, give the potatoes and yogurt a quick stir, then add lots of chopped fresh mint. Serve with warmed poppadoms.

*cook's tip

To cook poppadoms, heat about ¹/₂ inch/1 cm vegetable or peanut oil in a kadhai, wok, or large skillet. Add each poppadom and cook for a few seconds until it expands, turns pale golden brown, and small bubbles appear all over the surface. Use tongs to remove from the pan and drain on crumpled paper towels. Alternatively, preheat the broiler to its highest setting. Brush each poppadom with a little vegetable or peanut oil and broil for a few seconds on each side.

Intricate stone carvings are often used to depict Indian gods and stories

chicken tikka
murgh tikka

This is a quick version of the traditional tikka recipe (for a more authentic tandoori recipe, try the Tandoori Chicken on page 156). It uses boneless chicken thighs and captures the flavors of Indian cooking without resorting to a jar of sauce. The word "tikka" means that the dish is made from pieces of chicken or meat rather than a whole bird.

SERVES 4

4 skinless, boneless chicken thighs, cut into strips*

for the tikka paste

²/₃ cup plain yogurt

2 tbsp lemon juice

1 tbsp Garlic and Ginger Paste (see page 27)

1 tbsp tomato paste

2 tsp Garam Masala (see page 251)

seeds from 2 black cardamom pods

¹/₂ tsp ground cumin

¹/₂ tsp ground coriander

1 tsp paprika

¹/₂ tsp chili powder

salt

to serve

shredded iceberg lettuce

lemon wedges

1 To make the tikka paste, mix the yogurt, lemon juice, garlic and ginger paste, tomato paste, garam masala, cardamom seeds, cumin, coriander, paprika, chili powder, and salt to taste together in a nonmetallic bowl. Add the chicken pieces and stir them around so they are coated. Let the mixture marinate for 30 minutes at room temperature, or cover and chill for up to 24 hours.

2 Meanwhile, if you are using long, wooden skewers for this rather than metal ones, place 4 skewers upright in a tall glass of water to soak for 20 minutes so they do not burn under the broiler.

3 Preheat an oiled broiler to medium-high. If you have refrigerated the chicken, remove it from the refrigerator 15 minutes before broiling. Thread the chicken pieces on to 4 wooden or metal skewers.

4 Broil the chicken for 12–15 minutes, turning over once or twice and basting with any remaining marinade, until it is lightly charred and the juices run clear when it is pierced with a fork. Serve on the shredded lettuce with lemon wedges for squeezing over. Naans and chutneys make this into a filling first course.

*cook's tip
You can also use the paste with skinless, boneless chicken breasts or lamb fillet. Marinate the lamb for as long as possible, preferably overnight.

Overleaf *A general store, selling just about everything you could want, in Goa*

plantain chips
kele ke chips

What could be simpler? These plantain chips from Kerala are very moreish, so cook plenty. The bananas that grow abundantly in southern India are the small green ones that resemble plantains in the West, and you will find them in Indian or Caribbean food markets. They are delicious served straight from the pan with a chutney for dipping.

SERVES 4

4 ripe plantains*
1 tsp mild, medium, or hot curry powder, to taste
vegetable or peanut oil, for deep-frying
grated fresh coconut (optional)

1 Peel the plantains, then cut crosswise into ⅛-inch/ 3-mm slices. Put the slices in a bowl, sprinkle over the curry powder, and use your hands to toss them lightly together.

2 Heat enough oil for deep-frying in a kadhai, wok, deep-fat fryer, or large, heavy bottom pan to 350°F/180°C, or until a cube of bread browns in 30 seconds. Add as many plantain slices as will fit in the pan without overcrowding and cook for 2 minutes, or until golden.

3 Remove the plantain chips from the pan with a slotted spoon and drain well on crumpled paper towels. If you have a fresh coconut, use a fine grater to grate fresh flakes over the chips while they are still hot. Serve at once.

*cook's tip
Ordinary yellow-skinned bananas can also be used in this recipe, but the cooking will take a little less time.

An old man in traditional Indian dress plays a wooden instrument similar to a flute

60 paneer tikka
paneer tikka

For India's millions of vegetarians, paneer, this firm, white cheese, is the main source of dietary protein. It has very little taste on its own, which is why it is paired here with a hot, spicy tikka paste. The contrasting flavors produce a medium-hot dish that calls out for a cool beer.

SERVES 4

12 oz/350 g Paneer (see page 252), cut into 16 cubes

melted Ghee (see page 253) or vegetable or peanut oil, for brushing

1 tsp Garam Masala (see page 251)

fresh cilantro leaves, to garnish

for the tikka paste*

10 black peppercorns

6 cloves

seeds from 4 green cardamom pods

1 tsp cumin seeds

1 tsp coriander seeds

1/2 tsp poppy seeds

1/2 tsp chili powder

1/2 tsp ground turmeric

2 tbsp Garlic and Ginger Paste (see page 27)

1 wedge of onion, chopped

2/3 cup plain yogurt

1/2 tbsp tomato paste

1 tbsp besan or gram flour

1 tbsp vegetable or peanut oil

1 To make the tikka paste, dry-roast the peppercorns, cloves, and the cardamom, cumin, coriander, and poppy seeds in a hot skillet over high heat, stirring constantly, until you can smell the aromas. Immediately tip the spices out of the pan so they don't burn.

2 Put the spices in a spice grinder or mortar. Add the chili powder and turmeric and grind the spices to a fine powder. Add the garlic and ginger paste and onion and continue grinding until a paste forms. Transfer to a large bowl and stir in the yogurt, tomato paste, besan flour, and oil.

3 Add the paneer to the bowl and use your hands to coat the cubes in the tikka paste, taking care not to break up the pieces of cheese. Set aside for 30 minutes to marinate at room temperature, or cover the bowl with plastic wrap and chill for up to 24 hours.

4 Meanwhile, if you are using long, wooden skewers for this rather than metal ones, place 4 skewers upright in a tall glass of water to soak for 20 minutes so they do not burn under the broiler.

5 Preheat the broiler to medium-high. If you have refrigerated the cheese, remove it from the refrigerator 15 minutes before broiling. Lightly rub the 4 wooden or metal skewers with some oil. Thread the cheese cubes on to the skewers, leaving a little space between each cube.

6 Broil the skewers for 12–15 minutes, turning them over once and basting with any remaining tikka paste, until the cheese is lightly charred on the edges. Brush the hot kabobs with the melted ghee, sprinkle with garam masala, and garnish with cilantro leaves.

*cook's tips

To save time, replace the individual spices with 2 tablespoons bought tandoori masala spice mix, available from Indian food stores. Add the spice mix to the garlic and ginger paste in Step 2 and continue with the recipe.

These kabobs are good for a quick snack, but if you want something more filling for a main course, chop 2 cored and seeded red and/or yellow bell peppers into large cubes and quickly blanch in boiling water, then rinse in cold water. Thread the Paneer on to the skewers with alternating pieces of bell pepper and white mushrooms.

cocktail crab cakes
kekda tikki

Traditionally served as a savory teatime snack that young children enjoy with their mothers, these lightly spiced potato cakes are shaped into bite-size portions here to serve with cocktails, a chilled glass of beer, or a tall, cooling lassi.

MAKES 14

2 large baking potatoes, about 1 lb/450 g, scrubbed
   and cut in half

1/2 tsp ground turmeric

3 scallions, very finely chopped

1 fresh green chili, seeded and finely chopped

1/2-inch/1-cm piece fresh gingerroot, grated

2 tbsp finely chopped fresh cilantro leaves and stems

finely grated rind of 1 lemon

juice of 2 lemons

7 oz/200 g canned crabmeat, well-drained and flaked*

salt and pepper

vegetable or peanut oil, for frying

to serve

lemon or lime wedges

chutney or raita

1 Boil the potatoes in their skins in a large pan of lightly salted water until they are tender when poked with a fork. Drain well and peel when cool enough to handle.

2 Put the potato flesh in a large bowl and use a potato masher or fork to mash, but not until completely smooth. Add the turmeric and stir until it is well distributed. Stir in the scallions, chili, ginger, cilantro, lemon rind, and lemon juice to taste. Add the crabmeat and use your hands to work it into the potato mixture so that it is evenly distributed. Season to taste with salt and pepper.

3 Wet your hands and shape the potato mixture into 14 balls, then flatten each into a patty about 1 1/2 inches/4 cm across and 1/2 inch/1 cm wide.

4 Heat a thin layer of oil in a kadhai, wok, or large skillet over medium-high heat. Add as many potato cakes as will fit in a single layer without overcrowding the pan and cook for about 4 minutes until golden and crisp. Continue until all the potato cakes are cooked.

5 Serve the potato cakes warm or at room temperature, with lemon or lime wedges for squeezing over and a chutney or raita for dipping.

*cook's tip
You can substitute canned salmon or tuna for the crab.

Fishing off the coast of Kochi, southern India

64 onion and tomato salad
cachumber

This popular everyday Indian salad is typical of what is served in many restaurants. Teamed with Chapatis (see page 236), it makes a light meal on its own, or is an ideal accompaniment to serve with Lamb Biryani (see page 126) or any tandoori recipe. Only make it, however, when you have flavorsome sun-ripened tomatoes.

SERVES 4–6

3 tomatoes, seeded and chopped

1 large onion, finely chopped

3 tbsp chopped fresh cilantro, plus a little extra
 for garnishing

1–2 fresh green chilies, seeded and very finely sliced*

2 tbsp lemon juice

1 tsp salt

pinch of sugar

pepper

1 Put the tomatoes, onion, cilantro, and chilies in a bowl. Add the lemon juice, salt, sugar, and pepper to taste, then gently toss all together. Cover and chill for at least 1 hour.

2 Just before serving, gently toss the salad again. Add extra lemon juice or salt and pepper to taste. Spoon into a serving bowl and sprinkle with a little chopped cilantro.

*cook's tip

The searing heat in chilies that can make your mouth feel as if it is burning comes from a chemical called capsaicin, which is found in the seeds and veins. By seeding a chili you remove the heat, so the flavor can be enjoyed. To seed a chili, use a small, sharp knife to make a long slice in the chili from the stem end to the tip, then use the point of the knife to scrape out the seeds and veins.

gujarat carrot salad 65
gajar nu salat

In Gujarat in northwestern India, where this universally popular salad originated, the local carrots are a vibrant red-orange color.

SERVES 4–6

1 lb/450 g carrots, peeled

1 tbsp vegetable or peanut oil

$^1/_2$ tbsp black mustard seeds

$^1/_2$ tbsp cumin seeds

1 fresh green chili, seeded and chopped

$^1/_2$ tsp sugar

$^1/_2$ tsp salt

pinch of ground turmeric

1$^1/_2$–2 tbsp lemon juice

1 Grate the carrots on the coarse side of a grater into a bowl, then set aside.

2 Heat the oil in a kadhai, wok, or large skillet over medium-high heat. Add the mustard and cumin seeds and cook, stirring, until the mustard seeds start popping. Immediately remove the pan from the heat and stir in the chili, sugar, salt, and turmeric. Let the spices cool for about 5 minutes.

3 Pour the warm spices and any oil over the carrots and add the lemon juice. Toss together and adjust the seasoning, if necessary, then cover and chill for at least 30 minutes. Give the salad a good toss just before serving.

66 # malabar hill crab salad
eguru kosumalli

Mumbai's grandest homes are on Malabar Hill, an oasis well above the noisy hustle and bustle of the city with fantastic views over the bay. For the city's stylish ladies-who-lunch and Bollywood stars, this is typical of the refreshing salads enjoyed on cool palm- and flower-bedecked verandas.

SERVES 4–6

12 oz/350 g fresh cooked white crabmeat

3 scallions, finely chopped

2 tbsp roughly chopped fresh cilantro leaves

2 tbsp roughly chopped fresh mint leaves

salt and pepper

2 mangoes, finely chopped*

fresh cilantro sprigs, to garnish

lime wedges, to serve

for the dressing

2 oz/55 g creamed coconut

4 tbsp boiling water

1 fresh red chili, seeded and finely chopped

finely grated rind and juice of 1 lime

1 To make the dressing, crumble the creamed coconut into a large heatproof bowl and gradually stir in enough of the boiling water for the coconut to dissolve and form a thick liquid. Stir in the chili and lime rind and add lime juice to taste. Set aside until completely cool.

2 When the dressing is cool, stir in the crabmeat and scallions, then cover and chill until required.

3 When you are ready to serve, stir the cilantro and mint leaves into the salad. Add extra lime juice, if desired, and season to taste with salt and pepper. Add the mango and toss. Garnish with the cilantro sprigs and serve on individual plates, with lime wedges for squeezing over.

*cook's tip

If you've never handled a mango before, it can seem difficult to peel and pit because the slippery flesh clings to the flat pit in the center. Hold the unpeeled mango firmly on the counter with one hand and use a sharp knife to slice off one side, cutting as close to the pit as possible, then repeat on the other side. Cut a crisscross pattern in the flesh on each half, without cutting through the peel, then hold the flesh upward and gently bend the peel back, cutting out cubes of mango. Cut the flesh away from the pit in the leftover central piece.

chili chickpea salad
chatpate channe

1 Put the yogurt, red onion, and chili in a bowl and stir together. Stir in the chickpeas and set aside.

2 Heat the oil in a kadhai, wok, or large skillet over medium-high heat. Add the cumin seeds, mustard seeds, and asafoetida and stir for 1–2 minutes until the seeds jump and crackle.

3 Immediately tip the hot seeds into the chickpeas and stir around. Add lemon juice and salt and pepper to taste. The salad is now ready to eat, or it can be covered and chilled for up to a day. Serve sprinkled with the chopped fresh mint.

cook's tip

You can use dried chickpeas to make this flavorsome salad. Soak 1 cup dried chickpeas in plenty of water overnight. Drain, then place the chickpeas in a large pan with fresh water to cover and bring to a boil. Boil for 10 minutes, skimming the surface as necessary, then reduce the heat and let the chickpeas simmer for 1–1½ hours, depending on how old the chickpeas are (the older they are, the longer they will take to become tender). Do not add any salt until the chickpeas are tender. Drain well and add to the yogurt mixture in Step 1 of the recipe.

For the Punjabi Sikhs, dried chickpeas are a winter staple. Here chickpeas are made into a versatile salad, which can be enjoyed as a light appetizer or as part of a vegetarian meal with a selection of breads and raitas.

SERVES 4–6

4 tbsp plain yogurt

½ red onion, very finely chopped

½ fresh red chili, seeded or not, to taste, and finely sliced

14 oz/400 g canned chickpeas, rinsed and very well drained*

2 tsp vegetable or peanut oil

2 tsp cumin seeds

2 tsp black mustard seeds

pinch of ground asafoetida

1 tsp lemon juice

salt and pepper

chopped fresh mint, to garnish

68

memsahib's mulligatawny soup
mullagatanni

Mulligatawny is a taste of the Raj that still appears on restaurant menus throughout India. The name of this filling, spiced soup comes from a corruption of the Tamil "milagu tannir," which translates as "pepper water." Soups have never featured large in Indian cooking, so when the British arrived they adapted the Tamils' Rasam (see page 71) to this.

SERVES 4–6

3 tbsp Ghee (see page 253) or vegetable or peanut oil

2 large garlic cloves, crushed

2 carrots, diced

2 celery stalks, chopped

1 large onion, chopped

1 large dessert apple, peeled, cored, and chopped

1 tbsp besan or gram or all-purpose flour

1–2 tsp mild, medium, or hot curry powder, to taste

2 tsp ready-made curry paste

$1/2$ tsp ground coriander

1 quart vegetable, lamb, or chicken stock

2 large tomatoes, chopped

salt and pepper

$1/2$ cup cooked basmati rice (optional)

3 oz/85 g cooked beef, lamb, or skinless
   chicken, diced

chopped fresh cilantro, to garnish

1 Melt the ghee in a large pan or flameproof casserole over medium heat. Add the garlic, carrot, celery, onion, and apple and sauté for 5–8 minutes, stirring, until the onion just starts to brown.

2 Stir in the flour, curry powder, curry paste, and coriander and continue sautéing for an additional minute, stirring.

3 Stir in the stock and bring to a boil. Add the tomatoes and season to taste with salt and pepper, then reduce the heat, cover, and simmer for 45 minutes, or until the vegetables and apple are very tender.

4 Let the soup cool a little, then blend it in a food processor or blender until smooth. Use a wooden spoon to press the soup through a strainer into the rinsed pan, discarding any of the remains of the flavorings in the strainer.

5 Add the rice, if using, and stir in the beef, lamb, or chicken. Bring to a boil, then simmer for 5 minutes to heat the meat. Ladle into bowls and sprinkle with the cilantro.

Beautifully carved stonework in the holy southern town of Hampi

rasam

rasam

This traditional, light broth from Tamil Nadu is believed to be what the Raj cooks took and adapted into Memsahib's Mulligatawny Soup (see page 68). Leaving the seeds in the chili when you chop it adds an authentic burst of heat.

SERVES 4–6

1¹/₂ tbsp mustard oil

1 oz/30 g tamarind paste

1 quart hot water

1 large onion, chopped

4 large garlic cloves, chopped

1 fresh red chili, chopped

4 large tomatoes, seeded and chopped

1 tsp ground cumin

1 tbsp tomato paste (optional)

1 tbsp black mustard seeds

salt and pepper

fresh cilantro leaves, to garnish

1 Heat 1 tablespoon of the mustard oil in a large pan over high heat until it smokes. Remove the pan from the heat and let the oil cool. Meanwhile, put the tamarind paste in a bowl and stir in a scant 1 cup of the hot water, stirring to dissolve the paste.

2 Grind the onion, garlic, and chili into a paste in a spice blender, or use a pestle and mortar.

3 Return the pan with the mustard oil to medium-high heat. Add the onion paste and cook, stirring, for 2 minutes. Stir in the tomatoes, cumin, tamarind liquid, and remaining water.

4 Bring to a boil, then reduce the heat, cover, and simmer for 5 minutes. Taste and stir in the tomato paste if the tomatoes do not have enough flavor or color.

5 Meanwhile, heat the remaining mustard oil in a skillet. Add the mustard seeds and cook, stirring, for 1–2 minutes until they jump and crackle. Immediately tip the seeds out of the pan on to crumpled paper towels to drain, then set aside.

6 Let the soup cool a little, then process it in a food processor or blender until smooth. Use a wooden spoon to press the soup through a strainer into the rinsed pan, discarding the tomato seeds and skins remaining in the strainer.

7 Reheat the soup and add salt and pepper to taste. Ladle into bowls and sprinkle with the mustard seeds. Garnish with the cilantro and serve*.

*cook's tip
To transform this into a light vegetarian meal, serve it Tamil-style, ladled over rice.

72 turmeric yogurt soup
haldi dahi ka shorba

The zingy, vibrant yellow of this creamy vegetarian soup is the unmistakable hue of turmeric, used to color many Indian dishes. Grown in the large spice plantations of southern India, turmeric is used both in the kitchen and in the medicine cabinet as an antiseptic.

SERVES 4–6

generous ¹/₃ cup besan or gram flour

1 tsp ground turmeric

¹/₄ tsp chili powder

¹/₂ tsp salt

1³/₄ cups plain yogurt

2 tbsp Ghee (see page 253) or vegetable or peanut oil

3 cups water

for the garnish*

¹/₂ tbsp Ghee (see page 253) or vegetable or peanut oil

³/₄ tsp cumin seeds

¹/₂ tsp black mustard seeds

¹/₂ tsp fenugreek seeds

4–6 fresh red chilies, depending on how many
   you are serving

1 Mix the besan flour, turmeric, chili powder, and salt together in a large bowl. Use a whisk or fork and beat in the yogurt until no lumps remain.

2 Melt the ghee in a kadhai, wok, or heavy-bottom pan over medium-high heat. Mix in the yogurt mixture and then the water, whisking constantly. Bring to a boil, then reduce the heat to very low and simmer, still whisking frequently, for 8 minutes, or until the soup thickens slightly and doesn't have a "raw" taste any longer. Taste and stir in extra salt, if necessary.

3 In a separate small pan, melt the ghee for the garnish. Add the cumin, mustard, and fenugreek seeds and stir around until the seeds start to jump and crackle. Add the chilies, remove the pan from the heat, and stir for about 30 seconds, or until the chilies blister (if the chilies are fresh they might burst and "jump," so stand well back).

4 Ladle the soup into bowls and spoon the cooked spices over, including a little of the light brown ghee to serve.

*cook's tip
If you don't want to temper the spices (see pages 76–9) for the garnish, spoon a dollop of Cilantro Chutney (see page 245) into each portion instead.

VEGETABLE
DISHES

76

With the largest vegetarian population in the world, it isn't surprising that meatless cooking in India is unequaled in variety and flavors. Fresh vegetables, fruits, dried lentils, beans, and peas, grains, nuts, seeds, and dairy products provide endless nutritionally balanced meals and inspiration for Indian cooks.

The richness of Indian vegetarian cooking has evolved over centuries. Many of India's myriad religious and philosophical beliefs meet in vegetarianism. Although Hinduism only prohibits the consumption of beef, millions of Hindus abstain from eating any meat, and Jains and Buddhists, who abhor killing any living creatures, also eschew meat. The ancient traditions of Ayurveda, which promotes good health through herbal treatments and a vegetarian diet, is a way of life for millions. And, of course, so many Indians are vegetarians because the cost of meat can be prohibitive.

Few similarities exist between the culinary traditions of north and south India, but fine vegetarian cooking is one of them. Wherever one travels in India, there will always be a "veg" option at mealtimes, and even domestic airlines provide "veg" and "non-veg" meal options on all flights, regardless of how brief the journey is.

Indian vegetable markets are colorful displays of fresh produce. The country does not have a lot of refrigerated transportation or an integrated fast road or railroad network, so usually the fruits and vegetables for sale are local and seasonal. Growers transport and display their produce in wide, shallow

Wherever one travels in India, there will always be a "veg" option at mealtimes

baskets, each filled to the brim with only one ingredient, making it easier for eagle-eyed cooks to search out the best.

Dals are a regular feature of vegetarian meals everywhere in India. Dal is the word used to describe both the split dried lentils, beans, and peas and the numerous dishes prepared with split and whole dried lentils, beans, and peas. Dals provide the inexpensive backbone of most vegetarian meals and they are an excellent lowfat source of fiber. Also, many of the most popular Indian dried lentils, beans, and peas do not require presoaking or lengthy cooking, an obvious bonus for cooks when most Indians eat dal and rice at least once a day. *Dal roti*, or "dal and bread," is the subsistence food for millions every day.

Anyone new to dal cooking can find the choice of dals available in an Indian food store bewildering, not at all aided by the inconsistent labeling. The dals used in the recipes in this book include *chana dal* (split yellow lentils or husked Bengal gram), *masoor dal* (split red lentils), *urad dal chilke* (split black lentils or husked and split Egyptian lentils), *urad dal sabat* (whole black lentils), and *kabuli chana* (whole white chickpeas) and they are all available in Indian food stores.

The skill Indian cooks display in transforming otherwise dull-tasting and bland-looking lentils into appealing dishes with exciting flavors and varied texture can only be admired. One technique for flavoring dal is to pour hot oil with sautéed spices and leaves over the dish just before serving. This

1u11111

Another unique feature of Indian vegetarian cooking is the use of paneer

is called a *tarka*, or tempering, and is believed to bring the dish alive.

Another unique feature of Indian vegetarian cooking is the use of Paneer (see page 252), the creamy white pressed cheese. Like tofu from China, paneer is bland tasting on its own, but absorbs flavors from the other ingredients it is cooked with. Try Paneer Tikka (see page 60) or Matar Paneer (see page 100) for two different tastes of this very versatile ingredient.

Gujarat, the westernmost Indian state along the Arabian Sea, has a large Jain population who do not use onion or garlic as flavorings and it is considered the home of refined vegetarian cooking. Try Khandvi (see page 47), thin rolls of pie dough with a colorful *tarka* for a less-familiar Indian snack. Kitchri (see page 117), the original rice and lentil dish that Raj cooks transformed into kedgeree, is from there, as are the Golden Cauliflower Pakoras (see page 42).

All regions in India have traditional dishes to satisfy non-meat eaters. Try Spiced Pumpkin and Coconut (see page 88) from Bengal, Sambhar (see page 82) from the sunny south, Aloo Gobi (see page 103) from the north, and Tomato-Stuffed Eggplants (see page 94) from Maharashtra.

Dishes in other chapters that are ideal for including in vegetarian meals include Raita Potatoes (see page 52), Rasam (see page 71), and Turmeric Yogurt Soup (see page 72). Also, all the recipes in the Desserts & Drinks and the Accompaniments chapters help create a vegetarian feast that captures the delicious flavors of India. All the recipes in this chapter make a main dish-size portion.

Left *With no refrigeration, Indian stall-holders rely on shade to keep their produce cool*

Overleaf *A whole team of men is needed to pull these fishing boats up on to the beach*

sambhar
sambhar

This light, soup-like lentil curry from Tamil Nadu is probably the most typical dish of southern India. With a large vegetarian population in the region, most people will eat one version or another of this every day, starting with breakfast when it is often served with steamed rice cakes called idlis. *Chapatis (see page 236) are just as suitable.*

SERVES 4–6

1¼ cups split red lentils (masoor dal), rinsed

6 oz/175 g new potatoes, scrubbed and finely diced

1 large carrot, finely diced

1 green bell pepper, cored, seeded, and finely chopped

4 cups water

¼ tsp ground turmeric

¼ tsp ground asafoetida

1 tbsp tamarind paste or Tamarind Chutney
  (see page 249)

salt

for the sambhar masala*

3 dried red chilies, stems removed

2 tbsp coriander seeds

2 tsp cumin seeds

2 tsp black mustard seeds

1 tsp black peppercorns

1 tsp fenugreek seeds

3 cloves

¼ tsp ground turmeric

½ tsp ground asafoetida

1½ tsp vegetable or peanut oil

1½ tbsp split yellow lentils (chana dal)

1 tbsp dry unsweetened coconut

1½ tbsp split black lentils (urad dal chilke)

for the garnish

1½ tbsp vegetable or peanut oil

12 fresh curry leaves or 1 tbsp dried

2 dried red chilies

1 tsp black mustard seeds

1 Put the red lentils in a bowl with enough water to cover and let soak for 30 minutes, changing the water once.

2 To make the sambhar masala heat a kadhai, wok, or large skillet over medium-high heat. Add the chilies, coriander, cumin, and mustard seeds, peppercorns, fenugreek seeds, and cloves and dry-roast, stirring constantly, until the mustard seeds start to jump, you can smell the aromas, and the seeds darken in color, but do not burn. Stir in the turmeric and asafoetida, then immediately tip the spices into a bowl.

3 Return the pan to the heat. Add the oil and heat, then stir in the split yellow lentils, coconut, and split black lentils and cook for about 1 minute until they darken in color. Tip them out of the pan and add to the other spices.

4 Let the spice mixture cool completely, then place in a spice grinder, or use a pestle and mortar, and grind to a fine powder.

5 Drain the lentils. Put them in a kadhai, wok, or large skillet with the potatoes, carrot, and bell pepper and pour over the water. Bring to a boil, skimming the surface as necessary. Reduce the heat to the lowest setting, stir in the turmeric and asafoetida, and half cover the pan. Simmer, stirring occasionally, for 15–20 minutes until the vegetables and lentils are tender, but the lentils aren't falling apart.

6 Stir in the tamarind paste and 2 teaspoons of the sambhar masala. Taste and add extra masala and salt to taste. Continue simmering slowly while making the garnish.

7 To make the garnish, heat the oil in a large pan over high heat. Add the curry leaves, chilies, and mustard seeds and stir around quickly, standing back because they will splutter. Transfer the lentils to a serving dish and pour the hot oil and spices over.

*cook's tip

Unlike garam masala, which is the main flavoring mixture of northern dishes and is made from "hot" spices, sambhar masala is made from what are considered the "cool" spices, to temper the heat of southern India. It is impractical to make this in small quantities, so store the leftover masala in a sealed jar for up to 4 months, and use to flavor and thicken vegetable and lentil stews. If you don't want to go to the bother of making your own spice mixture, ready-made sambhar masala is sold in Indian food stores.

dosa masala
masala dosa

*The most popular snack in southern India, this is
a filling vegetarian feast. Thin, crisp, ghee-rich crêpes
called Dosas (see page 243) are rolled around a spicy
potato and tamarind mixture, an instant clue that
the dish comes from the south. Although this might
not instantly spring to mind when Westerners think
of "breakfast," this is often served to start the day.
If you are making the dosas, don't forget to begin
soaking the lentils and rice a day before, and make
the batter long enough in advance for it to ferment.
You can buy a package of dosa mix from Indian food
stores, but the results aren't as rich or crisp.*

MAKES 8

3 tbsp mustard oil*

2 tsp black mustard seeds

12 fresh curry leaves or 1 tbsp dried

3 fresh green chilies, seeded and chopped

1 1/2 large onions, chopped

1/2 tsp ground turmeric

1 lb 10 oz/750 g new potatoes, scrubbed and chopped

salt

2 cups water

1/2–1 tbsp tamarind paste or Tamarind Chutney
  (see page 249)

3/4 oz/20 g creamed coconut, grated and dissolved
  in 1 tbsp boiling water

chopped fresh cilantro

8 Dosas (see page 243), kept warm

selection of chutneys, to serve

1 Heat the mustard oil in a large skillet or pan with a
lid over high heat until it smokes. Turn off the heat
and let the mustard oil cool completely.

2 Reheat the mustard oil over medium-high heat. Add
the mustard seeds and stir until they start to jump.
Stir in the curry leaves, chilies, and onions and sauté,
stirring frequently, for 5–8 minutes until the onions are
soft, but not brown.

3 Stir in the turmeric, then add the potatoes and a
pinch of salt. Pour in the water and bring to a boil.
Reduce the heat to the lowest setting and simmer,
covered, for 12–15 minutes until the potatoes are very
tender and almost falling apart and most of the water
has evaporated. Stir in the tamarind paste and coconut,
add extra salt, if necessary, and stir in the cilantro.

4 One side of each dosa will be a smooth golden
brown and the other side will be more mottled.
Put one-eighth of the filling on the mottled side and
roll the dosa around it. Continue until all the dosas
are filled. Serve hot or at room temperature with a
selection of chutneys.

*cook's tip

Vegetable or peanut oil can replace the mustard oil.
If you do this, however, skip Step 1.

hot tomato raita
tamattar ka raita

This colorful and fragrant curry is similar to a warm raita and it goes exceptionally well with plain basmati rice. The inclusion of several varieties of chilies is an indication that it could have originated around Chennai. The spicy heat of the dish will be determined by whether or not the green chilies are seeded. The more seeds they contain, the hotter the dish will be.

SERVES 4–6

2 tbsp vegetable or peanut oil

1 tsp mustard seeds

7 oz/200 g shallots, finely sliced

1 tbsp Garlic and Ginger Paste (see page 27)

12 fresh curry leaves or 1 tbsp dried

2 dried red chilies

2 fresh green chilies, seeded or not, to taste,
  and chopped

$\frac{1}{2}$ tsp ground coriander

$\frac{1}{2}$ tsp ground turmeric

8 large, firm ripe tomatoes, about
  1 lb 5 oz/600 g, chopped

$1\frac{1}{2}$ tbsp tomato paste

$1\frac{1}{4}$ cups plain yogurt*

salt

chopped fresh mint, reserving sprig to garnish

1 Heat the oil in a kadhai, wok, or large skillet over medium-high heat. Add the mustard seeds and stir them around until they start to jump and crackle.

2 Stir in the shallots and garlic and ginger paste and stir for about 5 minutes until the shallots are golden.

3 Add the curry leaves, dried chilies, green chili, coriander, and turmeric, reduce the heat, and stir for 30 seconds.

4 Add the tomatoes and tomato paste to the pan and simmer for about 5 minutes, stirring gently, to soften and heat the tomatoes, but not to break them up completely.

5 Remove the pan from the heat and gradually stir in the yogurt, beating well after each addition. Taste and add salt if necessary. Cover the pan and let stand for 2–3 minutes, then stir gently. Sprinkle with the mint.

*cook's tip
If you taste various brands of plain yogurt they will differ in their sourness. If you find this dish too sour, stir in jaggery, an Indian sugar, or brown sugar.

spiced balti cabbage
bhuni pattagobhi

*A quick stir-fry dish that has grown out of the
tradition of Balti cooking.*

SERVES 4

2 tbsp vegetable or groundnut oil

¹/₂ tbsp cumin seeds

2 large garlic cloves, crushed

1 large onion, thinly sliced

1 lb 5 oz/600 g savoy cabbage, cored and thinly sliced

²/₃ cup Balti Sauce (see page 155)

¹/₄ tsp Garam Masala (see page 251)

salt

chopped fresh cilantro, to garnish

1 Heat the oil in a kadhai, wok, or large skillet over
   medium-high heat. Add the cumin seeds and stir
for about 80 seconds until they start to brown.

2 Immediately stir in the garlic and onion and sauté,
   stirring frequently, for 5–8 minutes until golden.

3 Add the cabbage* to the pan and stir for 2 minutes,
   or until it starts to wilt. Stir in the balti sauce and
bring to a boil, stirring. Reduce the heat a little and
simmer for 3–5 minutes until the cabbage is tender.

4 Stir in the garam masala and add salt to taste.
   Sprinkle with the cilantro.

*cook's tip
To make this into a more substantial, filling dish, add
14 oz/400 g drained and rinsed canned chickpeas with
the cabbage in Step 3.

88 spiced pumpkin and coconut
kaddu aur nariyal ki sabzi

SERVES 4–6

¹/₂ fresh coconut, about 4¹/₂ oz/125 g of flesh*

1 fresh green chili, seeded and chopped

1¹/₂ tsp sugar

1 tsp ground coriander

³/₄ tsp ground cumin

¹/₄ tsp chili powder

2 bay leaves

2 tbsp Ghee (see page 253) or vegetable or peanut oil

1 lb 5 oz/600 g pumpkin, peeled, seeded, and coarsely grated

1 tsp Garam Masala (see page 251)

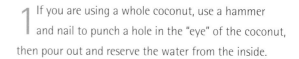

1 If you are using a whole coconut, use a hammer and nail to punch a hole in the "eye" of the coconut, then pour out and reserve the water from the inside.

2 Measure the coconut water and add water, if necessary, to make a generous 1 cup. Add the chili, sugar, coriander, cumin, chili powder, and bay leaves to the coconut water and set aside.

3 Use the hammer to break the coconut in half, then peel half and grate the flesh on the coarse side of a grater or whiz in a food processor (save the other half to use in another recipe, such as the Coconut Sambal on page 247).

4 Melt the ghee in a kadhai, wok, or large skillet over medium heat. Add the pumpkin and stir for 1 minute. Add the grated coconut and continue stirring until the mixture starts to turn brown.

5 Stir in the coconut water. Increase the heat and continue stir-frying until only about 4 tablespoons of liquid are left. Sprinkle with the garam masala and continue stir-frying until all the liquid has evaporated.

cook's tip
Before you buy a coconut, shake it. If you hear a lot of liquid slushing around inside, it is fresh. If you can't find a fresh coconut, use 1¹/₄ cups dry unsweetened coconut and stir-fry the pumpkin and coconut in a mixture of 4¹/₂ oz/125 g creamed coconut dissolved in a generous 1 cup boiling water.

parsi scrambled eggs
akoori

It isn't only Parsis who enjoy this spicy breakfast—this dish is popular throughout southern India and can be transformed into a tempting snack or lunch by serving it on pan-fried bread.

SERVES 4–6

6–8 eggs

4 tbsp light cream or milk

pinch of ground turmeric

salt and pepper

2 tbsp Ghee (see page 253) or vegetable or peanut oil

6 scallions, finely chopped

2 fresh green chilies, seeded and chopped

1/2-inch/1-cm piece fresh gingerroot,
   very finely chopped

2 tomatoes, seeded and finely chopped

4 tbsp finely chopped fresh cilantro

Parathas (see page 239), to serve

1 Crack the eggs into a small bowl and lightly beat, then mix in the cream, turmeric, and salt and pepper to taste.

2 Melt the ghee in a kadhai, wok, or large skillet over medium-high heat. Add the scallions, chilies, and ginger and stir around for 2–3 minutes until the scallions are starting to soften.

3 Add the tomatoes and stir around for 30 seconds. Add the egg mixture and half the cilantro and stir until the eggs are lightly set and creamy. Taste and adjust the seasoning, if necessary. Sprinkle with the remaining cilantro and serve with the parathas.

90

cauliflower, eggplant, and green bean korma
sabzi ka korma

Mild and fragrant, this slow-braised mixed vegetable dish reflects the skilled flavoring of Moghul cooking. The rich, almost velvety cream-based sauce is spiced but doesn't contain chilies, making it a rich treat for anyone who prefers mild dishes.

SERVES 4–6

generous ¹/₂ cup cashew nuts

1¹/₂ tbsp Garlic and Ginger Paste (see page 27)

scant 1 cup water

4 tbsp Ghee (see page 253) or vegetable or peanut oil

1 large onion, chopped

5 green cardamom pods, lightly crushed*

1 cinnamon stick, broken in half

¹/₄ tsp ground turmeric

generous 1 cup heavy cream

5 oz/140 g new potatoes, scrubbed and chopped into
  ¹/₂-inch/1-cm pieces

140 g/5 oz cauliflower florets

¹/₂ tsp Garam Masala (see page 251)

5 oz/140 g eggplant, chopped into chunks

5 oz/140 g green beans, chopped into ¹/₂-inch/1-cm pieces

salt and pepper

chopped fresh mint or cilantro, to garnish

1 Heat a large flameproof casserole or skillet with a tight-fitting lid over high heat. Add the cashew nuts and stir them around just until they start to brown, then immediately tip them out of the casserole.

2 Put the nuts in a spice blender with the garlic and ginger paste and 1 tablespoon of the water and whiz until a coarse paste forms.

3 Melt half the ghee in the casserole over medium-high heat. Add the onion and sauté for 5–8 minutes until golden brown.

4 Add the nut paste and stir for 5 minutes. Stir in the cardamom pods, cinnamon stick, and turmeric.

5 Add the cream and the remaining water and bring to a boil, stirring. Reduce the heat to the lowest level, cover the casserole, and simmer for 5 minutes.

6 Add the potatoes, cauliflower, and garam masala and simmer, covered, for 5 minutes. Stir in the eggplant and green beans and continue simmering for an additional 5 minutes, or until all the vegetables are tender. Check the sauce occasionally to make sure it isn't sticking on the bottom of the pan, and stir in extra water if needed.

7 Taste and add seasoning, if necessary. Sprinkle with the mint or cilantro.

*cook's tip
When you serve this, remember to tell guests that it contains cardamom pods, which have a bitter taste if bitten into.

chickpeas with spiced tomatoes
chhole tamattar

In the Punjab, chickpeas are popular all year round, and are often included in Sikh festive meals. Here they are made into a versatile salad that can be enjoyed as a light appetizer or as part of a vegetarian meal with a selection of breads and raitas.

SERVES 4–6

6 tbsp vegetable or peanut oil

2 tsp cumin seeds

3 large onions, finely chopped

2 tsp Garlic and Ginger Paste (see page 27)

2 small fresh green chilies, seeded and thinly sliced

1 1/2 tsp ground mango (amchoor powder)

1 1/2 tsp Garam Masala (see page 251)

3/4 tsp ground asafoetida

1/2 tsp ground turmeric

1/4–1 tsp chili powder

3 large, firm tomatoes, about 1 lb/450 g, grated*

1 lb 12 oz/800 g canned chickpeas, rinsed and drained

6 tbsp water

10 1/2 oz/300 g fresh spinach leaves, rinsed

1/2 tsp salt

1 Heat the oil in a kadhai, wok, or large skillet over medium-high heat. Add the cumin seeds and stir around for 30 seconds or until they brown and crackle, watching carefully because they can burn quickly.

2 Immediately stir in the onions, garlic and ginger paste, and chilies and sauté, stirring frequently, for 5–8 minutes until the onions are golden.

3 Stir in the ground mango, garam masala, asafoetida, turmeric, and chili powder. Add the tomatoes to the pan, stir them around, and continue cooking, stirring frequently, until the sauce blends together and starts to brown slightly.

4 Stir in the chickpeas and water and bring to a boil. Reduce the heat to very low and use a wooden spoon or a potato masher to mash about a quarter of the chickpeas, leaving the others whole.

5 Add the spinach to the pan with just the water clinging to the leaves and stir around until it wilts and is cooked. Stir in the salt, then taste and adjust the seasoning, if necessary.

*cook's tip
Grating tomatoes is an ingenious technique for eliminating the tough, curled pieces of tomato skins from a dish without having to go to the trouble of peeling the tomatoes first. Just rub the tomatoes firmly up and down on the coarse side of a standard box grater positioned over a bowl. The pulp will go into the bowl and you will be left with the skin and most of the core in your hand.

tomato-stuffed eggplants
bharwan baingan tamattari

94

From Maharashtra, this is an Indian technique for cooking whole, small eggplants with a thin layer of spicy stuffing between the slices. It is an excellent dish for entertaining because the fiddly work can be done well in advance.

MAKES 4

4 small eggplants, about 5 inches/13 cm long

Ghee (see page 253) or vegetable or peanut oil

for the stuffing

4 firm tomatoes, grated

2 onions, grated

2 fresh red chilies, seeded or not, to taste, and chopped

4 tbsp lemon juice

4 tbsp finely chopped fresh cilantro

1 tbsp Garlic and Ginger Paste (see page 27)

1¹/₂ tbsp ground coriander

2 tsp ground cumin

1 tsp fennel seeds

1 tsp ground turmeric

1 tsp salt

besan or gram flour (optional)

1 To make the stuffing, mix together the tomatoes, onions, chilies, lemon juice, cilantro, garlic and ginger paste, coriander, cumin, fennel seeds, turmeric, and salt in a nonmetallic bowl. The filling should not be stiff, but thick enough that it doesn't slide off the eggplant slices. If the tomatoes are very juicy and have made the filling too runny, gradually stir in about 1 tablespoon besan flour.

2 To prepare the eggplants, work with one at a time. Slit each one into 4 parallel slices, from top to bottom, without cutting through the stem end, so that the eggplant remains in one piece. Lightly fan the slices apart, then use a small spoon or your fingers to fill, dividing a fourth of the stuffing between the slices and covering each slice to the edges. Carefully layer the slices back into position so the eggplant looks whole again. Continue in the same way with the remaining eggplants*.

3 Choose a flameproof casserole or heavy-bottom skillet with a tight-fitting lid that is large enough to hold the eggplants in a single layer. Melt enough ghee to cover the bottom of the pan with a layer about ¹/₄ inch/5 mm deep. Add the eggplants in a single layer.

4 Put the pan over the lowest heat and cover tightly. Let cook for 15 minutes, then carefully turn the eggplants over. Re-cover the pan and continue cooking for an additional 10–15 minutes, or until the eggplants are tender when you pierce them with a skewer or a knife. Check occasionally while the eggplants are cooking, and if they start to stick to the bottom of the pan, stir in a couple of tablespoons of water. Serve hot or at room temperature.

*cook's tip
This simple dish looks very attractive fanned on a plate for individual servings. For a buffet or party, however, vertically cut the eggplants into ¹/₂-inch/1-cm slices. The slices look as though they are from a layered vegetable terrine, but with much less work.

Overleaf The stunning red buildings of the desert city of Jodhpur in Rajasthan

Punjabi cooks took this recipe with them when they left India after the Partition and now it is an Indian restaurant favorite around the world. For the millions of Hindu vegetarians in northern India, however, it remains a regular and important source of protein. Saag is a Hindi word meaning "greens," and although this is most commonly made with spinach outside India, in India it might include mustard greens, beet greens, or whatever is available.

spinach and paneer   99
saag paneer

SERVES 4

3 oz/85 g Ghee (see page 253) or 6 tbsp vegetable
  or peanut oil

12 oz/350 g Paneer (see page 252), cut into
  ¹/₂-inch/1-cm pieces

1¹/₂ tbsp Garlic and Ginger Paste (see page 27)

1 fresh green chili, seeded or not, to taste,
  and chopped

4 tbsp water

1 onion, finely chopped

1 lb 5 oz/600 g fresh spinach leaves, any thick stems
  removed and rinsed

¹/₄ tsp salt

¹/₄ tsp Garam Masala (see page 251)

4 tbsp heavy cream

lemon wedges, to serve

1 Melt the ghee in a flameproof casserole or large skillet with a tight-fitting lid over medium-high heat. Add as many paneer pieces as will fit in a single layer without overcrowding the casserole and pan-fry for about 5 minutes until golden brown on all sides. Use a slotted spoon to remove the paneer and drain it on crumpled paper towels. Continue, adding a little extra ghee, if necessary, until all the paneer is cooked.

2 Put the garlic and ginger paste and chili in a spice grinder or mortar and grind until a thick paste forms. Add the water and blend again.

3 Reheat the casserole with the ghee. Stir in the onion with the garlic and ginger paste mixture and sauté, stirring frequently, for 5–8 minutes until the onion is soft, but not brown.

4 Add the spinach with just the water clinging to the leaves and the salt and stir around until it wilts. Reduce the heat to low, cover the casserole, and continue simmering until the spinach is very soft.

5 Stir in the garam masala and cream, then gently return the paneer to the casserole*. Simmer, stirring gently, until the paneer is heated through. Taste and adjust the seasoning, if necessary. Serve with lemon wedges for squeezing over.

*cook's tip
For a variation, stir 1 or 2 large seeded and chopped tomatoes into the spinach with the paneer in Step 5.

100

matar paneer
mattar paneer

This is another popular Indian restaurant dish from Punjabi cooks. The sweetness of the peas contrasts well with the richness of the paneer.

SERVES 4

3 oz/85 g Ghee (see page 253) or 6 tbsp vegetable
   or peanut oil

12 oz/350 g Paneer (see page 252), cut into
   $^1/_2$-inch/1-cm pieces*

2 large garlic cloves, chopped

$^1/_2$-inch/1-cm piece fresh gingerroot, finely chopped

1 large onion, finely sliced

1 tsp ground turmeric

1 tsp Garam Masala (see page 251)

$^1/_4$–$^1/_2$ tsp chili powder

3 cups frozen peas or 1 lb 5 oz/600 g fresh
   peas, shelled

1 fresh bay leaf

$^1/_2$ tsp salt

$^1/_2$ cup water

chopped fresh cilantro, to garnish

1 Heat the ghee in a large skillet or flameproof casserole with a tight-fitting lid over medium-high heat. Add as many paneer pieces as will fit in a single layer without overcrowding the pan and pan-fry for about 5 minutes until golden brown on all sides. Use a slotted spoon to remove the paneer and drain on crumpled paper towels. Continue, adding a little extra ghee, if necessary, until all the paneer is cooked.

2 Reheat the pan with the ghee. Stir in the garlic, ginger, and onion and sauté, stirring frequently, for 5–8 minutes until the onion is soft, but not brown.

3 Stir in the turmeric, garam masala, and chili powder and sauté for an additional 2 minutes.

4 Add the peas, bay leaf, and salt to taste to the pan and stir around. Pour in the water and bring to a boil. Reduce the heat to very low, then cover and simmer for 10 minutes, or until the peas are tender.

5 Gently return the paneer to the pan. Simmer, stirring gently, until the paneer is heated through. Taste and adjust the seasoning, if necessary. Sprinkle with cilantro.

*cook's tip
If you make the paneer for this dish, save a generous $^1/_3$ cup of the whey and use it to replace the water in Step 4.

Although many Indian women enjoy Western fashion, most prefer to wear traditional Indian dress

There must be as many versions of this popular
north Indian dry dish as there are cooks. This is
an excellent accompaniment to all tandoori recipes.

aloo gobi 103
aloo gobi

SERVES 4-6

4 tbsp Ghee (see page 253) or vegetable or peanut oil

1/2 tbsp cumin seeds

1 onion, chopped

1 1/2-inch/4-cm piece fresh gingerroot, finely chopped

1 fresh green chili, seeded and thinly sliced

1 lb/450 g cauliflower, cut into small florets

1 lb/450 g large waxy potatoes, peeled and cut into
large chunks

1/2 tsp ground coriander

1/2 tsp Garam Masala (see page 251)

1/4 tsp salt

fresh cilantro sprigs, to garnish

1 Melt the ghee in a flameproof casserole or large
skillet with a tight-fitting lid over medium-high
heat. Add the cumin seeds and stir around for about
30 seconds until they crackle and start to brown.

2 Immediately stir in the onion, ginger, and chili and
stir for 5-8 minutes until the onion is golden.

3 Stir in the cauliflower and potatoes, followed by the
coriander, garam masala, and salt and continue
stirring for about 30 seconds longer*.

4 Cover the pan, reduce the heat to the lowest
setting, and simmer, stirring occasionally, for
20-30 minutes until the vegetables are tender when
pierced with the point of a knife. Check occasionally
that they aren't sticking to the bottom of the pan and
stir in a little water, if necessary.

5 Taste and adjust the seasoning, if necessary, and
sprinkle with the cilantro to serve.

*cook's tip
For a more golden-colored dish, add 1/4 teaspoon ground
turmeric with the other ground spices in Step 3.

*A young girl helps with the
household chores*

104 # madras potatoes
madrasi aloo

Madras Potatoes ... Bombay Potatoes ... similar potato recipes to this appear on most Indian restaurant menus under a variety of names. Waxy potatoes are the best to use because they hold their shape during the rapid sautéing, but mealy potatoes are fine as long as you don't mind a texture that is almost falling apart.

SERVES 4–6

2 lb/900 g new potatoes, scrubbed and
  cut into halves or fourths

salt

3 tbsp Ghee (see page 253) or vegetable or peanut oil

2 tsp black mustard seeds

1 onion, sliced

4 garlic cloves, very finely chopped

1-inch/2.5-cm piece fresh gingerroot,
  very finely chopped

1 fresh red chili, seeded or not, to taste,
  and finely chopped

1 tsp ground cumin

$^{1}/_{2}$ tsp ground coriander

chopped fresh cilantro, to garnish

lemon wedges, to serve

1 Put the potatoes in a large pan of salted boiling water over high heat and bring to a boil, then boil for 5–8 minutes, or until tender when pierced with the point of a knife. Drain well, then set aside to cool.

2 Melt the ghee in a kadhai, wok, or large skillet over medium-high heat. Add the mustard seeds and stir them around for about 1 minute until they start to crackle and jump.

3 Mix in the onion and sauté, stirring frequently, for 5 minutes, then stir in the garlic, ginger, and chili and continue cooking until the onion is golden.

4 Add the cumin and coriander and stir around until well blended.

5 Add the potatoes and stir until they are hot and coated with spices. Add extra salt, if necessary. Sprinkle with the chopped cilantro and serve with the lemon wedges*.

*cook's tip
Served at room temperature with an ice-cold beer or a Salt Lassi (see page 212), these make a good *chaat*, or snack. Just serve with toothpicks for picking up.

106 okra bhaji
bhindi ki sabzi

Okra, called "ladies' fingers" or bhindi *in India, is one of those ingredients that people either devour or shun, usually because the cut pods are cooked in liquid to produce a slimy texture. This quick northern Indian method of stir-frying the crisp green pods eliminates that problem.*

SERVES 4

3 tbsp Ghee (see page 253) or vegetable or peanut oil

1 onion, thinly sliced

1 lb 2 oz/500 g okra, stem ends trimmed off

1 or 2 fresh green chilies, seeded or not,
  to taste, and sliced

2 tsp ground cumin

salt and pepper

¹/₄ tsp Garam Masala (see page 251)

lemon wedges, to serve

1 Melt the ghee in a kadhai, wok, or large skillet over medium-high heat. Add the onion and sauté, stirring frequently, for 2 minutes.

2 Add the okra, chilies, cumin, and salt and pepper to taste and continue cooking, stirring, for 5 minutes.

3 Sprinkle with the garam masala and continue stirring about 2 minutes longer until the okra are tender, but still crisp*. Serve with lemon wedges.

*cook's tip
For a variation, add 2 seeded and chopped tomatoes with the okra and chili or remove the pan from the heat when the okra is tender and slowly stir in a generous 1 cup plain yogurt, a little at a time, beating constantly.

chili-yogurt mushrooms
mushroom dahiwale

*Here is another Indian restaurant favorite that is
quick and easy to make at home. If you think of
mushrooms as bland and uninteresting, think again.
The recipe uses cremini mushrooms, but white
mushrooms can be used instead.*

SERVES 4–6

4 tbsp Ghee (see page 253) or vegetable or peanut oil

2 large onions, chopped

4 large garlic cloves, crushed

14 oz/400 g canned chopped tomatoes

1 tsp ground turmeric

1 tsp Garam Masala (see page 251)

¹/₂ tsp chili powder

1 lb 10 oz/750 g cremini mushrooms, thickly sliced

pinch of sugar

salt

¹/₂ cup plain yogurt

chopped fresh cilantro, to garnish

1 Melt the ghee in a kadhai, wok, or large skillet over
medium-high heat. Add the onion and sauté,
stirring frequently, for 5–8 minutes until golden. Stir
in the garlic and sauté for an additional 2 minutes.

2 Add the tomatoes and their juice and mix around.
Stir in the turmeric, garam masala, and chili powder
and continue cooking for an additional 3 minutes.

3 Add the mushrooms, sugar, and salt*, to taste, and
cook for about 8 minutes until they have given off
their liquid and are soft and tender.

4 Turn off the heat, then stir in the yogurt, a little
at a time, beating vigorously to prevent it curdling.
Taste and adjust the seasoning, if necessary. Sprinkle
with cilantro and serve.

*cook's tip
Adding the salt with the mushrooms in Step 3 draws
out their moisture, giving extra flavor to the juices.

green beans with mustard seeds and coconut

frans bean raiwali

This is a popular southern Indian way to serve beans. It is lightly spiced, so it makes a perfect accompaniment to hot curry dishes.

SERVES 4–6

3 tbsp Ghee (see page 253) or vegetable or peanut oil

1 tbsp mustard seeds

6 fresh curry leaves or ¹/₂ tbsp dried

1 onion, chopped

¹/₂ tbsp Garlic and Ginger Paste (see page 27)

pinch of ground turmeric

1 lb/450 g green beans, trimmed and chopped

2 oz/55 g creamed coconut, grated

generous 1 cup water

salt and pepper

pinch of chili powder or paprika, to serve

1 Melt the ghee in a kadhai, wok, or large skillet over high heat. Add the mustard seeds and stir around for about a minute until they pop. Stir in the curry leaves.

2 Add the onion, garlic and ginger paste*, and turmeric and stir for 5 minutes. Add the green beans and stir for 2 minutes.

3 Sprinkle in the creamed coconut, then add the water and bring to a boil, stirring. Reduce the heat to low and simmer, stirring occasionally, for about 4 minutes until the beans are tender, but still have some bite. Taste and adjust the seasoning and sprinkle with a little chili powder to serve.

*cook's tip
If you like your vegetable dishes with more heat, add 1 chopped fresh green chili with the garlic and ginger paste in Step 2.

In rural India, animals are important members of the workforce

110 spinach and lentils
palak daal

Vegetarian Indian cooks never seem to run out of ideas for flavorful, quick, everyday meals that combine lentils or dried beans or peas with vegetables. Chana dal are ideal for this simple style of dish because they don't require lengthy soaking or cooking.

SERVES 4

1¹/₄ cups split yellow lentils (chana dal), rinsed

1 quart water*

1 tsp ground coriander

1 tsp ground cumin

¹/₄ tsp ground asafoetida

¹/₂ tsp ground turmeric

9 oz/250 g fresh spinach leaves, thick stems removed, sliced and rinsed

4 scallions, chopped

salt

for the garnish

3 tbsp vegetable or peanut oil

1 tsp mustard seeds

2 fresh green chilies, split lengthwise

¹/₂-inch/1-cm piece fresh gingerroot, very finely chopped

1 Put the lentils and water in a large pan over high heat. Bring to a boil, reduce the heat to the lowest setting, and skim the surface as necessary.

2 When the foam stops rising, stir in the coriander, cumin, asafoetida, and turmeric. Half cover and let the lentils continue simmering for about 40 minutes, or until very tender and only a thin layer of liquid is left on top.

3 Stir the spinach and scallions into the lentils and continue simmering for an additional 5 minutes, stirring frequently, until the spinach is wilted. If the water evaporates before the spinach is cooked, stir in a little extra. Add salt to taste. Transfer the lentils to a serving dish.

4 For the garnish, heat the oil in a small pan over high heat. Add the mustard seeds, chilies, and ginger and stir around until the mustard seeds begin to pop and the chilies sizzle. Pour the oil and spices over the lentils to serve.

*cook's tip

The exact amount of water needed depends primarily on how old the lentils are, but also on the size of the pan. The older the lentils are, the longer simmering they will require to become tender. Unfortunately, there isn't any way to determine the age when you buy lentils, so be prepared to add extra water and increase the cooking time in Step 2. Also, remember the wider the pan, the quicker the water will evaporate.

Using whole black lentils with their skins still on rather than split lentils adds a gelatinous texture to this rich dal. This dish is time-consuming to prepare, so it is more likely to be served in restaurants or for special occasions than on an everyday basis.

black dal 113
maah ki daal

SERVES 4–6

1¼ cups whole black lentils (urad dal sabat)

⅔ cup dried red kidney beans

4 garlic cloves, cut in half

4 black cardamom pods, lightly crushed

2 bay leaves

1 cinnamon stick

4 oz/115 g butter

1½ tbsp Garlic and Ginger Paste (see page 27)

2 tbsp tomato paste

½ tsp chili powder

pinch of sugar

salt

⅔ cup heavy cream

fresh cilantro sprigs, to garnish

1 Put the lentils and beans in separate bowls with plenty of water to cover and let soak for at least 3 hours, but ideally overnight.

2 Meanwhile, put the garlic cloves, cardamom pods, bay leaves, and cinnamon stick in a piece of cheesecloth and tie together into a bundle.

3 Drain the lentils and beans separately. Put the beans in a kadhai, wok, or large pan with twice their volume of water and bring to a boil, then boil for 10 minutes and drain well.

4 Return the beans to the pan, add the lentils, and cover with double their volume of water. Add the spice bag and bring to a boil over high heat, then reduce the heat to low and simmer*, partially covered, for about 3 hours, skimming the surface as necessary, until the lentils and beans are very tender and reduced to a thick paste. Mash against the side of the pan with a wooden spoon or a potato masher every 15 minutes while they are simmering.

5 When the lentils and beans are almost cooked, remove the spice bag and set aside to cool. Melt the butter in a small pan. Add the garlic and ginger paste and stir around for 1 minute. Stir in the tomato, chili powder, sugar, and salt to taste and continue simmering for 2–3 minutes.

6 When the spice bag is cool enough to handle, squeeze all the flavoring juices into the lentils and beans. Stir the butter and spice mixture into the lentils and beans, along with all but 2 tablespoons of the cream. Bring to a boil, then reduce the heat and simmer for 10 minutes, stirring occasionally.

7 Transfer the dal to a serving dish, then swirl with the remaining cream and sprinkle with the cilantro sprigs.

*cook's tip
Watch the lentils and beans closely while they are simmering in Step 4, and stir in extra water if it evaporates before they are tender.

114 sweet-and-sour lentils
khatti meethi daal

This is the Bengali style of preparing yellow lentils.

SERVES 4

1¼ cups split yellow lentils (chana dal)

1 quart water

2 bay leaves, torn

3 fresh chilies, sliced once, but left whole

½ tsp ground turmeric

½ tsp ground asafoetida

3 tbsp vegetable or peanut oil

½ onion, finely chopped

¾-inch/2-cm piece fresh gingerroot, finely chopped

1 oz/30 g creamed coconut, grated

1 fresh green chili, seeded or not, to taste,
  and chopped

1½ tbsp sugar

1½ tbsp tamarind paste or Tamarind
  Chutney (see page 249)

½ tsp Garam Masala (see page 251)

¼ tsp ground cumin

¼ tsp ground coriander

salt*

to garnish

1 tbsp Ghee (see page 253), melted, or
  vegetable or peanut oil

1 tsp Garam Masala (see page 251)

chopped fresh cilantro

1 Put the lentils and water in a large pan with a lid over high heat and bring to a boil, skimming the surface as necessary. When the foam stops rising, stir in the bay leaves, chilies, turmeric, and asafoetida. Half cover the pan and let the lentils continue simmering for about 40 minutes, or until they are very tender, but not reduced to a mush, and all the liquid has been absorbed.

2 When the lentils are almost tender, heat the oil in a kadhai, wok, or large skillet over medium-high heat. Add the onion and ginger and sauté, stirring frequently, for 5–8 minutes.

3 Stir in the coconut, green chili, sugar, tamarind paste, garam masala, cumin, and coriander and stir around for about 1 minute.

4 When the lentils are tender, add them, the bay leaves, chilies, and any liquid left in the pan to the spice mixture and stir around to blend together. Taste and add salt, if necessary, and extra sugar and tamarind, if desired.

5 Transfer the lentils to a serving dish and drizzle the hot ghee over the top. Sprinkle with garam masala and cilantro.

**cook's tip*

Neither lentils nor any dried beans or peas should be seasoned with salt until after they are tender. If salt is added too soon, it will draw out any moisture so the lentils remain too dehydrated to digest easily.

kitchri
khichdee

This recipe makes a light meal on its own, served with hot bread and a raita, but it is also excellent to team with other vegetarian dishes. This is the traditional Indian dish that British cooks of the Raj adapted into kedgeree.

SERVES 4–6

scant 1¼ cups basmati rice

2 tbsp Ghee (see page 253) or vegetable or peanut oil

1 large onion, finely chopped

1¼ cups split red lentils (masoor dal), rinsed*

2 tsp Garam Masala (see page 251)

1½ tsp salt

pinch of ground asafoetida

3½ cups water

2 tbsp chopped fresh cilantro

to serve

Chapatis (see page 236)

Raita (see page 244)

1 Rinse the basmati rice in several changes of water until the water runs clear, then let soak for 30 minutes. Drain and set aside until ready to cook.

2 Melt the ghee in a flameproof casserole or large pan with a tight-fitting lid over medium-high heat. Add the onion and sauté for 5–8 minutes, stirring frequently, until golden, but not brown.

3 Stir in the rice and lentils along with the garam masala, salt, and asafoetida, and stir for 2 minutes. Pour in the water and bring to a boil, stirring.

4 Reduce the heat to as low as possible and cover the pan tightly. Simmer without lifting the lid for 20 minutes until the grains are tender and the liquid is absorbed. Re-cover the pan, turn off the heat, and let stand for 5 minutes.

5 Use 2 forks to mix in the cilantro and adjust the seasoning, if necessary. Serve with chapatis and raita.

*cook's tip

It's useful to keep a supply of lentils in the pantry as, unlike dried beans and peas, they do not need lengthy soaking before cooking. When you buy them in the supermarket they will be ready to use straight from the package, but if you buy them loose in Asian or health food stores, pick them over and rinse them to remove any grit. Lentils that have been on the shelf for a long time might take longer to cook.

MEAT & POULTRY DISHES

120

Almost any meat dish other than those served in a hotel in India can give some indication of the host's religious background. Meat-eating Hindus and Sikhs abstain from ever eating beef, and Muslims and kosher Jews do not touch pork. Christians and Parsis, on the other hand, eat all forms of meat, restricted only by expense.

Against this background of intertwined religion and food, the humble goat has emerged as the most popular red meat eaten in India. One piece of Indian folklore maintains that skilled northern Indian cooks can prepare a different goat dish for each day of the year. The exception is in Kashmir, where sheep graze on the mountains to make meat meltingly tender.

As traditional Indian recipes have been exported to Indian restaurants around the world, goat has been replaced with lamb, which is the meat used for recipes in this book. Chicken, regarded as an everyday meat in many other countries, might be scrawny-looking in India, but it is for the most part free-range and considered a choice treat, especially by Punjabi Hindus who serve it for wedding banquets and other large celebrations.

Meat features more in the daily diet of the northern states of Rajasthan, the Punjab, and Kashmir than elsewhere in India, and it is the northern Indian meat dishes that are most recognized outside the country. This is because it was Punjabis who opened the first Indian restaurants abroad and brought with them the rich tradition of Moghul cooking that has thrived since the last great invasion of the sixteenth century.

Tandoori cooking is one of the lasting legacies of the Moghul dynasties

Tandoori cooking is one of the lasting legacies of the Moghul dynasties. The tradition of cooking meat, poultry, fish, and to a lesser extent vegetables in a tall, charcoal-heated clay oven called a *tandoor* originated in northeastern Persia, and the technique has remained unchanged in the intervening centuries. Food, which is often first tenderized in a yogurt marinade, is cooked from the dry heat at the bottom and from the reflected heat of the sides. Lamb and chicken kabobs are particularly suited to this method. It is impossible to re-create the authentic flavors of tandoori cooking without a *tandoor* oven, but the Tandoori Chicken (see page 156) and Chicken Tikka (see page 55) recipes give similar results. Cilantro Lamb Kabobs (see page 133) is another tandoori-style recipe adapted for domestic ovens.

The Moghul court cooks also brought with them rich recipes, incorporating creamy sauces, spices, sweet fresh and plump dried fruits, and tender nuts. Moghul cooking reached its height with the rice and meat biryanis of the Nizam's royal kitchens in Hyderabad. Cooks here were unrivaled in their lavish, refined cooking. Lamb Biryani (see page 126) is a dish for celebrations, if only because it is time-consuming to prepare, but worth the effort for the subtle flavoring, wonderful aromas, and tenderness. The golden saffron finish alludes to its regal origins.

To sample other meat and poultry dishes that have evolved from Moghul kitchens, try Butter Chicken (see page 158) and Kashmiri Chicken (see page 162).

Cauliflower, Eggplant, and Green Bean Korma (see page 90) is a mild and rich vegetarian dish in the Moghul style.

Parsis, who fled persecutions in Persia centuries ago, are also meat-eaters, and their Persian heritage is reflected in rich and subtly flavored dishes. Try Lamb Dhansak (see page 138) to sample a thick, smooth sauce made from disintegrating lentils and pumpkin.

Hot and spicy Pork Vindaloo (see page 148) from Goa's Christian community is probably the country's best-known pork recipe. This tongue-tingling dish, generously flavored with fresh chilies as well as garlic and vinegar, reflects the years of Portuguese rule. Although vindaloos appear on restaurant menus made with beef and lamb, the pork version is authentic.

All meats, including pork, feature in Anglo-Indian cooks' repertoires. Anglo-Indian food is a hybrid of the bland food of the British Raj and traditional spiced Indian dishes, very much like the Indian food served in restaurants a decade or so ago. Try the Anglo-Indian Railroad Pork and Vegetables (see page 147) and the traditional Kheema Matar (see page 151) to see how the styles differ. Both are made with ground meat and are ideal for family meals, but completely different.

Authentic Indian meat and poultry recipes often require lengthy cooking to tenderize the meat to the point where it can be pulled into bite-size pieces with the fingers, and often meat is not taken off the bones during cooking, which adds extra flavor. The recipes in this book, however, require less cooking because they are intended to be eaten with knives and forks, and many recipes use boneless meat for convenience of cooking and preparation.

Overleaf *Palm trees are an important source of food in the south, providing oil, coconut meat, and milk*

126

lamb biryani
gosht biryani

From the Moghul courts of Hyderabad, this elaborate combination of rice and meat remains the Indian dish of choice for non-vegetarian weddings and celebrations.

SERVES 6–8

3 tbsp Ghee (see page 253) or vegetable or peanut oil

2 lb 4 oz/1 kg boneless leg of lamb, trimmed, patted dry, and cut into 2-inch/5-cm pieces

salt and pepper

1¼ large onions, finely chopped

1½ tbsp Garam Masala (see page 251)

½ tsp cumin seeds

1 cinnamon stick, broken in half

1-inch/2.5-cm piece fresh gingerroot, finely chopped

3 large garlic cloves, crushed

½ tsp ground turmeric

½ tsp chili powder

3 cups chicken stock

1 oz/30 g fresh cilantro leaves

2½ cups basmati rice

6 tbsp milk

1 tsp saffron threads

⅔ cup plain yogurt

to garnish

¾ large onion, finely sliced

1 tsp salt

4 tbsp vegetable or peanut oil

⅔ cup golden raisins

⅔ cup blanched almonds

3 hard-cooked eggs, halved lengthwise

chopped fresh cilantro

1 Melt 2 tbsp of the ghee in a large flameproof casserole over medium-high heat. Add the lamb, season well, and brown on all sides, then transfer to a plate. Work in batches, if necessary.

2 Wipe out the casserole and melt the remaining ghee over medium heat. Add the chopped onions and sauté, stirring frequently, for 5–8 minutes until soft and golden, but not brown. Stir in the garam masala, cumin seeds, and cinnamon stick and continue sautéing, stirring, for 2–3 minutes until you can smell the aromas.

3 Return the lamb and all its juices to the casserole. Add the ginger, garlic, turmeric, and chili powder and stir around for 3 minutes, or until you can smell the aromas. Add the stock and cilantro and bring to a boil. Reduce the heat to the lowest setting, cover the casserole, and let simmer for 1½ hours (the lamb should not be completely tender at this point).

4 Meanwhile, prepare the rice, milk, and garnish. Rinse the rice in several changes of cold water until the water is clear, then set the rice aside to soak for 20 minutes in plenty of water to cover.

5 To make the saffron milk, heat the milk until it simmers in a small pan, crumble in the saffron, and set aside to steep.

6 To make the dark onion garnish, put the sliced onion in a bowl, sprinkle with the salt, and let stand for about 5 minutes to extract the moisture. Use your hands to squeeze out the moisture. Heat half the oil in a skillet over high heat. Add the onion and sauté, stirring constantly, for 4–6 minutes until golden brown. Immediately tip out of the pan as it will continue to darken as it cools (if you wait until the onion is dark brown before you remove from the pan, it will develop a burned taste). Set the onion aside*.

7 Wipe out the skillet and melt the remaining oil in it. Add the golden raisins and fry, stirring, for 3–5 minutes until they are golden brown, then

immediately remove them from the pan with a slotted spoon. Add the almonds to the fat remaining in the pan and stir them around for 2–3 minutes until they turn golden brown, watching carefully because they can burn in seconds.

8 After the rice has soaked, drain it. Bring a large pan of water to a boil. Add the rice and cook for 5 minutes (it will not be completely tender at this point.) Drain well and set aside.

9 Preheat the oven to 375°F/190°C. Take the lamb off the heat and stir in the yogurt, a little at a time, stirring very fast to prevent it curdling. Adjust the seasoning.

10 Spoon the partially cooked rice over the lamb, mounding it up. Use the handle of a wooden spoon to make a hole in the center of the rice, moving the spoon around until the hole is about 1 inch/2.5 cm wide. Drizzle the saffron milk over the rice in "spokes" coming out from the center.

11 Cover the casserole and bake for 40 minutes. Remove the casserole from the oven and let stand for 5 minutes without lifting the lid.

12 Uncover the casserole and sprinkle the golden raisins and almonds over the top. Add the browned onion slices and hard-cooked eggs and sprinkle with cilantro. Serve straight from the casserole.

*cook's tip
A biryani dish like this is time-consuming to prepare, but Steps 1–6 can be done a day in advance.

rogan josh 129
rogan josh

Originally from Kashmir, this fragrant rich dish was quickly adopted by Moghul cooks and has remained a firm favorite in northern India ever since. A Kashmiri natural dye called rattanjog *traditionally provided the characteristic red color, but chili powder and tomato paste provide a more readily available, and less expensive, alternative in this recipe.*

SERVES 4

1¹/₂ cups plain yogurt

¹/₂ tsp ground asafoetida dissolved in 2 tbsp water

1 lb 9 oz/700 g boneless leg of lamb, trimmed and cut into 2-inch/5-cm cubes

2 tomatoes, seeded and chopped

1 onion, chopped

2 tbsp Ghee (see page 253) or vegetable or peanut oil

1¹/₂ tbsp Garlic and Ginger Paste (see page 27)

2 tbsp tomato paste

2 bay leaves

1 tbsp ground coriander

¹/₄–1 tsp chili powder, ideally Kashmiri chili powder*

¹/₂ tsp ground turmeric

1 tsp salt

¹/₂ tsp Garam Masala (see page 251)

1 Put the yogurt in a large bowl and stir in the dissolved asafoetida. Add the lamb and use your hands to rub in all the marinade, then set aside for 30 minutes.

2 Meanwhile, put the tomatoes and onion in a food processor or blender and whiz until blended. Melt the ghee in a flameproof casserole or large skillet with a tight-fitting lid. Add the garlic and ginger paste and stir around until you can smell cooked garlic.

3 Stir in the tomato mixture, tomato paste, bay leaves, coriander, chili powder, and turmeric, reduce the heat to low, and simmer, stirring occasionally, for 5–8 minutes.

4 Add the lamb and salt with any leftover marinade and stir around for 2 minutes. Cover, reduce the heat to low, and simmer, stirring occasionally, for 30 minutes. The lamb should give off enough moisture to prevent it catching on the bottom of the pan, but if the sauce looks too dry, stir in a little water.

5 Sprinkle the lamb with the garam masala, re-cover the pan, and continue simmering for 15–20 minutes until the lamb is tender when poked with a fork. Adjust the seasoning, if necessary.

*cook's tip
For an authentic flavor, search out the bright-red Kashmiri chili powder sold at Indian food stores.

130

lamb pasanda
gosht pasanda

This recipe is a legacy from the glorious days of the Moghul courts, when Indian cooking reached a refined peak. This rich, creamy dish gets its name from the word "pasanda," which indicates small pieces of boneless meat, in this case tender lamb, flattened as thin as possible.

SERVES 4–6

1 lb 5 oz/600 g boneless lamb shoulder or leg

2 tbsp Garlic and Ginger Paste (see page 27)

4 tbsp Ghee (see page 253) or vegetable or peanut oil

3 large onions, chopped

1 fresh green chili, seeded and chopped (optional)

2 green cardamom pods, lightly crushed

1 cinnamon stick, broken in half

2 tsp ground coriander

1 tsp ground cumin

1 tsp ground turmeric

generous 1 cup water

²/₃ cup heavy cream

4 tbsp ground almonds

1¹/₂ tsp salt

1 tsp Garam Masala (see page 251)

to garnish

paprika

toasted slivered almonds*

1 Cut the meat into thin slices, then place the slices between plastic wrap and bash with a rolling pin or meat mallet to make them even thinner. Put the lamb slices in a bowl, add the garlic and ginger paste, and use your hands to rub the paste into the lamb. Cover and set aside in a cool place to marinate for 2 hours.

2 Melt the ghee in a flameproof casserole or large skillet with a tight-fitting lid over medium-high heat. Add the onions and chili and sauté, stirring frequently, for 5–8 minutes until the onions are golden brown.

3 Stir in the cardamom pods, cinnamon stick, coriander, cumin, and turmeric and continue stirring for 2 minutes, or until the spices are aromatic.

4 Add the meat to the pan and cook, stirring occasionally, for about 5 minutes until it is brown on all sides and the fat begins to separate. Stir in the water and bring to a boil, still stirring. Reduce the heat to its lowest setting, cover the pan tightly, and simmer for 40 minutes, or until the meat is tender.

5 When the lamb is tender, stir the cream and almonds together in a bowl. Beat in 6 tablespoons of the hot cooking liquid from the pan, then gradually beat this mixture back into the casserole. Stir in the salt and garam masala. Continue to simmer for an additional 5 minutes, uncovered, stirring occasionally.

6 Garnish with a sprinkling of paprika and toasted slivered almonds to serve.

*cook's tip
To toast slivered almonds, put them in a dry skillet over medium heat and stir constantly until they turn golden brown. Immediately tip them out of the pan because they can burn quickly. Alternatively, toast them in a preheated oven, 350°F/180°C, on a cookie sheet for 10–15 minutes until golden.

cilantro lamb kabobs

gosht hara kabab

As you walk through any bazaar or market in a northern Indian city, street vendors will cook these fragrant and subtly spiced kabobs to order. They are cooked in a tandoor *oven to produce a dry exterior that keeps the center tender, but using a hot preheated broiler or cooking over glowing coals also gives good results.*

MAKES 4–6 SKEWERS

1 lb 9 oz/700 g ground lamb

1 onion, grated

3 tbsp finely chopped fresh cilantro leaves and stems

3 tbsp finely chopped fresh mint

3 tbsp besan or gram flour

1 1/2 tbsp ground almonds

1-inch/2.5-cm piece fresh gingerroot, grated

3 tbsp lemon juice

2 tbsp plain yogurt

2 tsp ground cumin

2 tsp ground coriander

1 1/2 tsp salt

1 1/2 tsp Garam Masala (see page 251)

1 tsp ground cinnamon

pepper, to taste

to serve

lemon wedges

salad

1 Place all the ingredients in a large bowl and use your hands to incorporate everything until the texture is smooth. Cover the bowl with a dish towel and let stand for about 45 minutes at room temperature.

2 With wet hands, divide the ground lamb mixture into 24 equal balls*. Working with one ball at a time, mold it around a long, flat metal skewer, shaping it into a cylinder shape. Continue until all the mixture has been used and you have filled 4 to 6 skewers.

3 Preheat the broiler to its highest setting or light barbecue coals and let burn until they turn gray. Lightly brush the broiler rack or barbecue grid with oil. Add the skewers and broil for 5–7 minutes, turning frequently, until the lamb is completely cooked through and not at all pink when you pierce it with the point of a knife. Serve with lemon wedges for squeezing over and a salad.

*cook's tip

If you don't want to be bothered shaping the lamb mixture into skewers, form 6 patties. Broil as above, but increase the cooking time to 4 minutes on each side.

134 sesame lamb chops
champ tilwale

In much of India, these chops, with their fragrant crunchy coating, would be made with young goat, but lamb is ideal. The brief marinating period tenderizes the meat, and flattening the meat speeds up the cooking time.

SERVES 4

12 lamb chops, such as blade or rib

1¹/₂ tbsp sesame seeds*

pepper

lime wedges, to serve

for the marinade

4 tbsp plain yogurt

2 tbsp grated lemon rind

1¹/₂ tsp ground cumin

1¹/₂ tsp ground coriander

¹/₄ tsp chili powder

salt

1 To make the marinade, put the yogurt, lemon rind, cumin, coriander, chili powder, and salt to taste in a large bowl and stir together.

2 Use a sharp knife to trim any fat from the edge of the lamb chops and scrape the meat off the long piece of bone. Using a rolling pin or the end of a large chef's knife, pound each chop until it is about ¹/₄ inch/5 mm thick.

3 Add the chops to the bowl and use your hands to stir around until they are coated in the marinade. Let marinate for 20 minutes at room temperature, or cover the bowl and refrigerate for up to 4 hours.

4 If the chops have been chilled, remove them from the refrigerator 20 minutes before broiling. Preheat the broiler to its highest setting and lightly grease the broiler rack.

5 Arrange the chops on the broiler rack in a single layer, then sprinkle the sesame seeds over each. Broil the chops about 4 inches/10 cm from the heat for about 7 minutes, without turning, for medium.

6 To serve, grind fresh pepper over the chops and serve with lime wedges for squeezing over.

*cook's tip

For a variation, omit the sesame seeds and spread a dollop of Coconut Sambal (see page 247) over the top of each chop before broiling.

lamb dopiaza
gosht dopiaza

When you see "dopiaza" in a recipe title, you can be certain it will contain lots of onions and, in fact, two types. "Do" literally means "two," and "piaza" means "onion." Some recipes will fold in raw onions toward the end of cooking for a crunchy texture, but both sliced and chopped onions are cooked in this very rich version.

SERVES 4–6

2 large onions, finely sliced

salt

2 large onions, coarsely chopped

2 tbsp Garlic and Ginger Paste (see page 27)

1/2 tsp ground paprika

2 tbsp chopped fresh cilantro

1 tbsp ground coriander

1 tsp ground cumin

1/2 tsp ground asafoetida

2 1/2 oz/70 g Ghee (see page 253) or 5 tbsp vegetable
   or peanut oil

1 lb 9 oz/700 g boneless shoulder of lamb, trimmed and
   cut into 2-inch/5-cm cubes

4 green cardamom pods

pinch of sugar

1/2 tsp Garam Masala (see page 251)

fresh cilantro sprigs, to garnish

1 Put the sliced onions in a bowl, sprinkle with 1 teaspoon salt, and let stand for about 5 minutes to extract the moisture. Use your hands to squeeze out the moisture.

2 Meanwhile, grind the chopped onions with the garlic and ginger paste, paprika, cilantro, coriander, cumin, and asafoetida in a spice blender or with a pestle and mortar.

3 Melt 2 tablespoons of the ghee in a flameproof casserole or large skillet with a tight-fitting lid over medium-high heat. Add the prepared sliced onions and sauté, stirring constantly, for 4–6 minutes until they are golden brown. Immediately tip them out of the pan as they will continue to darken as they cool (if you tip them out when they are brown, they will develop a burned taste).

4 Melt 2 tablespoons of the remaining ghee in the casserole. Add the lamb and brown on all sides, working in batches if necessary, then remove from the pan.

5 Melt the remaining ghee in the casserole. Add the onion paste and cook, stirring occasionally. Add the cardamom pods and stir around.

6 Return the lamb to the casserole and stir in 1/2 teaspoon salt and the sugar. Reduce the heat to very low, cover the casserole, and simmer for 30 minutes*.

7 Uncover the casserole and sprinkle the reserved onion slices and the garam masala over the lamb, re-cover the pan, and continue simmering for an additional 15 minutes, or until the lamb is tender. Taste and adjust the seasoning, if necessary. Sprinkle with cilantro sprigs.

*cook's tip

There should be enough moisture in the lamb to prevent the sauce from becoming too thick and catching on the bottom of the casserole in Step 6, but check occasionally and stir in a little water, if necessary.

138

lamb dhansak
gosht dhansak

*For India's numerous Parsis, this rich dish is served
for a Sunday family lunch. The lentils and pumpkin
dissolve into a velvety-smooth sauce, and all that
is needed to complete the meal are rice and naans.*

SERVES 4–6

1 lb 9 oz/700 g boneless shoulder of lamb, trimmed
and cut into 2-inch/5-cm cubes

salt

1 tbsp Garlic and Ginger Paste (see page 27)

5 green cardamom pods

1 cup yellow lentils (toor dal)

3¹/₂ oz/100 g peeled, seeded, and chopped pumpkin

1 carrot, thinly sliced

1 fresh green chili, seeded and chopped

1 tsp fenugreek powder

scant 2¹/₂ cups water

1 large onion, thinly sliced

2 tbsp Ghee (see page 253) or vegetable or peanut oil

2 garlic cloves, crushed

chopped fresh cilantro or mint, to garnish

for the dhansak masala*

1 tsp Garam Masala (see page 251)

¹/₂ tsp ground coriander

¹/₂ tsp ground cumin

¹/₂ tsp chili powder

¹/₂ tsp ground turmeric

¹/₄ tsp ground cardamom

¹/₄ tsp ground cloves

1 Put the lamb and 1 teaspoon salt in a large pan
with enough water to cover and bring to a boil.
Reduce the heat and simmer, skimming the surface as

necessary until no more foam rises. Stir in the garlic
and ginger paste and cardamom pods and continue
simmering for a total of 30 minutes.

2 Meanwhile, put the lentils, pumpkin, carrot, chili,
and fenugreek powder in a large, heavy-bottom
pan and pour over the water. Bring to a boil, stirring
occasionally, then reduce the heat and simmer for
20–30 minutes until the lentils and carrot are very
tender. Stir in a little extra water if the lentils look as
though they will catch on the bottom of the pan.

3 Let the lentil mixture cool slightly, then pour it into
a food processor or blender and whiz until a thick,
smooth sauce forms.

4 While the lamb and lentils are cooking, put the
onion in a bowl, sprinkle with 1 teaspoon salt,
and let stand for about 5 minutes to extract the
moisture. Use your hands to squeeze out the moisture.

5 Melt the ghee in a flameproof casserole or large
skillet with a tight-fitting lid over high heat. Add
the onion and sauté, stirring, for 2 minutes. Remove
one-third of the onion and continue sautéing the rest
for an additional 1–2 minutes until golden brown.
Immediately take a slotted spoon and remove the
remaining onion, as it will continue to darken as it cools.

6 Return the one-third of the onion to the pan with
the garlic. Stir in all the dhansak masala ingredients
and cook for 2 minutes, stirring constantly. Add the
cooked lamb and stir for an additional 2 minutes. Add
the lentil sauce and simmer over medium heat to warm
through, stirring and adding a little extra water, if
needed. Adjust the seasoning, if necessary. Sprinkle with
the dark onion and serve with cilantro sprinkled over.

*cook's tip
Look in Indian food stores for packages of ready-made
dhansak masala. Add 1 tablespoon to the onion in
Step 6 and continue with the recipe as above.

lamb with cauliflower
gobhi gosht   141

In the Punjab, this simple dish would most likely be made with tougher pieces of goat or mutton that require lengthy simmering to become tender, but when made with lamb neck fillets, as here, this makes a quick meal.

SERVES 4–6

2 tbsp Ghee (see page 253) or vegetable or peanut oil

1 onion, chopped

½ tbsp Garlic and Ginger Paste (see page 27)

1 tbsp cumin seeds

2 tsp mild, medium, or hot curry paste, to taste

1 head cauliflower, broken into small florets*

14 oz/400 g canned chopped tomatoes

½ cup vegetable stock or water

salt and pepper

1 lb 9 oz/700 g lamb neck fillet, trimmed and cut into
  ¼-inch/5-mm slices

lemon juice, to taste

chopped fresh mint, to garnish

1 Melt the ghee in a kadhai, wok, or large skillet over medium-high heat. Add the onion and garlic and ginger paste and sauté, stirring frequently, for 5–8 minutes until the onion is lightly browned.

2 Add the cumin seeds and curry paste and stir around for about 1 minute. Add the cauliflower and continue stirring for an additional minute.

3 Add the tomatoes with their juice, the stock, and salt and pepper to taste. Bring to a boil, then reduce the heat and simmer for 10 minutes, stirring occasionally, until the sauce is reduced and the tomatoes break down.

4 Add the lamb and continue simmering, stirring occasionally, for 10 minutes, or until it is tender and just pink in the center. Add lemon juice to taste and adjust the seasoning, if necessary. Serve garnished with a generous amount of mint.

*cook's tip

For a variation, substitute ½-inch/1-cm chunks of carrot or broccoli florets for the cauliflower. The broccoli, however, will only require about 5 minutes cooking in Step 3.

India has a high birthrate, and everywhere you go, children gather to welcome you

142 # lamb shanks marathani
ghati gosht

From Mumbai, this dish is bursting with lots of flavors that reflect the city's vibrancy and diversity. It's not for nothing that the port city is known as "The Gateway to India," as traders from all corners of the globe have always sold their wares here. "Marathani" in a recipe title indicates that a dish comes from the state of Maharashtra, of which Mumbai is the capital.

SERVES 4

4 tbsp Ghee (see page 253) or vegetable or peanut oil

2 large onions, thinly sliced

generous ¹/₄ cup cashew nuts

1¹/₂ tbsp Garlic and Ginger Paste (see page 27)

2 fresh green chilies, seeded and chopped

2 cinnamon sticks, broken in half

¹/₂ tsp chili powder

¹/₂ tsp ground turmeric

¹/₂ tsp ground coriander

¹/₄ tsp ground mace

3 tbsp plain yogurt

4 lamb shanks

3¹/₂ cups water

¹/₂ tsp Garam Masala (see page 251)

salt and pepper

chopped fresh cilantro, to garnish

Overleaf The Ganges River at Varanasi is one of India's most holy places

1 Melt half the ghee in a large flameproof casserole over medium-high heat. Add the onions and sauté, stirring frequently, for 5–8 minutes until soft but not colored. Stir in the cashew nuts and stir around for just 1–2 minutes until they turn light brown.

2 Use a slotted spoon to remove the onions and nuts from the casserole and let cool slightly. Transfer both to a food processor or mortar and grind until a paste forms and the nuts are well ground.

3 Melt the remaining ghee in the casserole. Add the garlic and ginger paste, chilies, and cinnamon sticks and stir around for about 1 minute until you can smell the aromas.

4 Stir in the chili powder, turmeric, coriander, and mace. Gradually stir in the yogurt, stirring constantly. Add the lamb shanks and continue stirring for about 5 minutes until the yogurt is absorbed.

5 Stir in the reserved onion and cashew paste. Pour in enough water to cover the lamb shanks, add the garam masala, and bring to a boil. Reduce the heat to low, cover the casserole, and let simmer for 1³/₄–2 hours until the lamb is very tender and almost falling off the bones*.

6 Taste and adjust the seasoning, if necessary. Serve the lamb shanks with the thin sauce spooned over and some chopped cilantro.

*cook's tip

The sauce, or "gravy" as Indians would say, with this dish is very thin. If you prefer a thicker sauce, transfer the lamb shanks to the oven at the end of Step 5. Stir 4 tablespoons of the sauce into 4 tablespoons rice flour to make a smooth paste. Stir the paste into the casserole, bring the sauce to a boil, and boil, stirring, for about 10 minutes until reduced and thickened.

148 pork vindaloo
gosht vindaloo

This dish is not for the faint-hearted! The name "vindaloo" comes from the Portuguese words for "vinegar" and "garlic," and this traditional Goan dish contains both. The dish's characteristic searing heat, however, comes from the chilies, which the Portuguese introduced along with vinegar when they conquered Goa in 1510. The Portuguese continued to rule this part of western India until it was annexed by India in 1961. One legacy of the Portuguese rule is a large Christian community, which eats pork, unlike many Hindus or Muslims.

SERVES 4–6

4 tbsp mustard oil

2 large onions, finely chopped

6 fresh bay leaves

6 cloves

6 garlic cloves, chopped

3 green cardamom pods, lightly cracked

1–2 small fresh red chilies, chopped

2 tbsp ground cumin

$\frac{1}{2}$ tsp salt

$\frac{1}{2}$ tsp ground turmeric

2 tbsp cider vinegar

2 tbsp water

1 tbsp tomato paste

1 lb 9 oz/700 g boneless shoulder of pork, trimmed
  and cut into 2-inch/5-cm cubes

1 Put the mustard oil in a large skillet or pan with a tight-fitting lid over high heat until it smokes. Turn off the heat and let the mustard oil cool completely.

2 Reheat the oil over medium-high heat. Add the onions and sauté, stirring frequently, for 5–8 minutes until soft but not colored.

3 Add the bay leaves, cloves, garlic, cardamom pods, chilies, cumin, salt, turmeric, and 1 tablespoon of the vinegar to the onions and stir around. Stir in the water, then cover the pan and simmer for about 1 minute, or until the water is absorbed and the fat separates.

4 Dissolve the tomato paste in the remaining tablespoon of vinegar, then stir it into the pan. Add the pork and stir around.

5 Add just enough water to cover the pork and bring to a boil. Reduce the heat to its lowest level, cover the pan tightly, and simmer for 40–60 minutes until the pork is tender.

6 If too much liquid remains in the pan when the pork is tender, use a slotted spoon to remove the pork from the pan and boil the liquid until it reduces to the required amount. Return the pork to heat through and adjust the seasoning, if necessary.

kheema matar
kheema mattar

When the cold winter winds come to northern India, this simple, rustic dish makes a popular family meal.

SERVES 4–6

2 tbsp Ghee (see page 253) or vegetable or peanut oil

2 tsp cumin seeds

1 large onion, finely chopped

1 tbsp Garlic and Ginger Paste (see page 27)

2 bay leaves

1 tsp mild, medium, or hot curry powder, to taste

2 tomatoes, cored, seeded, and chopped

1 tsp ground coriander

$^1/_4$–$^1/_2$ tsp chili powder

$^1/_4$ tsp ground turmeric

pinch of sugar

$^1/_2$ teaspoon salt

$^1/_2$ teaspoon pepper

1 lb 2 oz/500 g lean ground beef or lamb

$2^1/_4$ cups frozen peas, straight from the freezer

1 Heat the ghee in a flameproof casserole or large skillet with a tight-fitting lid. Add the cumin seeds and cook, stirring, for 30 seconds, or until they start to crackle.

2 Stir in the onion, garlic and ginger paste, bay leaves, and curry powder and continue to stir-fry until the fat separates.

3 Stir in the tomatoes and cook for 1–2 minutes. Stir in the coriander, chili powder, turmeric, sugar, salt, and pepper and stir around for 30 seconds.

4 Add the beef and cook for 5 minutes, using a wooden spoon to break up the meat, or until it is no longer pink. Reduce the heat and simmer, stirring occasionally, for 10 minutes.

5 Add the peas and continue simmering for an additional 10–15 minutes until the peas are thawed and hot. If there is too much liquid left in the pan, increase the heat and let it bubble for a few minutes until it reduces.

Many Indians are very interested in politics and photos of political figures are often seen hanging in public places

152

beef madras
madrasi gosht

This spicy curry with a hint of coconut gets its Indian name from the southeastern coastal town of Chennai, formerly known as Madras. The regional specialties are typically flavored with coconut and lots of chilies, which is why restaurant menus frequently label every hot dish as "Madras." Drink chilled beer or a Salt Lassi (see page 212) with this.

SERVES 4–6

1–2 dried red chilies*

2 tsp ground coriander

2 tsp ground turmeric

1 tsp black mustard seeds

½ tsp ground ginger

¼ tsp ground pepper

5 oz/140 g creamed coconut, grated and dissolved in
   1¼ cups boiling water

4 tbsp Ghee (see page 253) or vegetable or peanut oil

2 onions, chopped

3 large garlic cloves, chopped

1 lb 9 oz/700 g lean stewing steak, trimmed and cut
   into 2-inch/5-cm cubes

generous 1 cup beef stock

lemon juice

salt

1 Depending on how hot you want this dish to be, chop the chilies with or without any seeds. The more seeds you include, the hotter the dish will be. Put the chopped chili and any seeds in a small bowl with the coriander, turmeric, mustard seeds, ginger, and pepper and stir in a little of the coconut mixture to make a thin paste.

2 Melt the ghee in a flameproof casserole or large skillet with a tight-fitting lid over medium-high heat. Add the onions and garlic and sauté for 5–8 minutes, stirring often, until the onion is golden brown. Add the spice paste and stir around for 2 minutes, or until you can smell the aromas.

3 Add the meat and stock and bring to a boil. Reduce the heat to its lowest level, cover tightly, and simmer for 90 minutes, or until the beef is tender when you poke it with a fork. Check occasionally that the meat isn't catching on the bottom of the pan and stir in a little extra water or stock, if necessary.

4 Uncover the pan and stir in the remaining coconut milk with the lemon juice and salt to taste. Bring to a boil, stirring, then reduce the heat again and simmer, still uncovered, until the sauce reduces slightly.

*cook's tip
The dish takes on a different character, but is equally flavorsome, if you omit the chilies altogether and garnish the dish with toasted coconut flakes just before serving.

balti beef
bhuna gosht

Direct from Birmingham, England, this is the Indian/Pakistan version of stir-frying. Immigrants introduced "Brummies" to this quick style of cooking and now balti restaurants thrive throughout the UK and Europe. It's quick cooking once you've made the balti sauce, but that can be made in advance and refrigerated for several days.

SERVES 4–6

2 tbsp Ghee (see page 253) or vegetable or peanut oil

1 large onion, chopped

2 garlic cloves, crushed

2 large red bell peppers, cored, seeded, and chopped

1 lb 5 oz/600 g boneless beef for stir-frying, such as sirloin, thinly sliced

for the balti sauce

2 tbsp Ghee (see page 253) or vegetable or peanut oil

2 large onions, chopped

1 tbsp Garlic and Ginger Paste (see page 27)

14 oz/400 g canned chopped tomatoes

1 tsp ground paprika

$^1\!/_2$ tsp ground turmeric

$^1\!/_2$ tsp ground cumin

$^1\!/_2$ tsp ground coriander

$^1\!/_4$ tsp chili powder

$^1\!/_4$ tsp ground cardamom

1 bay leaf

salt and pepper

1 To make the balti sauce, melt the ghee in a kadhai, wok, or large skillet over medium-high heat. Add the onions and garlic and ginger paste and stir-fry for about 5 minutes until the onions are golden brown. Stir in the tomatoes with their juice, then add the paprika, turmeric, cumin, coriander, chili powder, cardamom, bay leaf, and salt and pepper to taste. Bring to a boil, stirring, then reduce the heat and simmer for 20 minutes, stirring occasionally.

2 Let the sauce cool slightly, then remove the bay leaf and pour the mixture into a food processor or blender and whiz to a smooth sauce.

3 Wipe out the kadhai, wok, or skillet and return it to medium-high heat. Add the ghee and melt. Add the onion and garlic and stir-fry for 5–8 minutes until golden brown. Add the red bell peppers and continue stir-frying for 2 minutes.

4 Stir in the beef and continue stirring for 2 minutes until it starts to turn brown. Add the balti sauce and bring to a boil. Reduce the heat and simmer for 5 minutes, or until the sauce slightly reduces again and the bell pepper is tender. Adjust the seasoning, if necessary, and serve in a kadhai.

156 tandoori chicken
tandoori murgh

Don't expect to duplicate this dish exactly as it is served at your favorite Indian restaurant. That's impossible to do at home—unless you happen to have a tandoor oven in the kitchen—but this comes close, especially if you let the bird marinate for a day before cooking. Indian cooks add the bright red-orange color to tandoori dishes with natural food colorings, such as cochineal. A few drops of red and yellow food coloring are a more readily available option for most home cooks, although it's not necessary. Kashmiri chili powder will also enhance the red color.

Indian village life is centered around agriculture and tied to the surrounding villages and cities

SERVES 4

1 chicken, weighing 3 lb 5 oz/1.5 kg, skinned*

¹/₂ lemon

1 tsp salt

2 tbsp Ghee (see page 253), melted

lemon wedges, to serve

for the tandoori masala paste

1 tbsp Garlic and Ginger Paste (see page 27)

1 tbsp ground paprika

1 tsp ground cinnamon

1 tsp ground cumin

¹/₂ tsp ground coriander

¹/₄ tsp chili powder, ideally Kashmiri chili powder

pinch ground cloves

¹/₄ tsp edible red food coloring (optional)

few drops of edible yellow food coloring (optional)

generous ³/₄ cup plain yogurt

1 To make the tandoori masala paste, combine the garlic and ginger paste, dry spices, and food coloring in a bowl and stir in the yogurt. You can use the paste now or store it in an airtight container in the refrigerator for up to 3 days.

2 Use a small knife to make thin cuts over the chicken. Rub the lemon half all over the chicken, then rub the salt into the cuts.

3 Put the chicken in a deep bowl, add the paste, and use your hands to rub it all over the bird and into the cuts. Cover the bowl with plastic wrap and refrigerate for at least 4 hours, but ideally up to 24 hours.

4 When you are ready to cook the chicken, preheat the oven to 400°F/200°C. Put the chicken on a rack in a roasting pan, breast-side up, and dribble with the melted ghee. Roast for 45 minutes, then quickly remove the bird and roasting pan from the oven and turn the temperature to its highest setting.

5 Very carefully pour out any fat from the bottom of the roasting pan. Return the chicken to the oven and roast for an additional 10–15 minutes until the chicken's juices run clear when you pierce the thigh with a knife and the paste is lightly charred.

6 Let stand for 10 minutes, then cut into pieces to serve with lemon wedges for squeezing over.

*cook's tip

For a quicker version, use chicken breasts, thighs, or drumsticks. Marinate as above, preheat the oven to 450°F/230°C, and roast for about 40 minutes.

158 butter chicken
murgh makhani

Like Chicken Tikka Masala (see page 161), the quickest way to prepare this popular Sikh dish is to buy ready-cooked tandoori chicken. Otherwise, start with the Tandoori Chicken recipe (see page 156). This is a good party dish, with a rich, creamy sauce that you can make as hot as you like, depending on the amount of chili powder you include.

SERVES 4–6

1 onion, chopped

1¹/₂ tbsp Garlic and Ginger Paste (see page 27)

14 oz/400 g large, juicy tomatoes, peeled and chopped, or canned tomatoes

¹/₄–¹/₂ tsp chili powder

pinch of sugar

salt and pepper

2 tbsp Ghee (see page 253) or vegetable or peanut oil

¹/₂ cup water

1 tbsp tomato paste

3 tbsp butter, cut into small pieces

¹/₂ tsp Garam Masala (see page 251)

¹/₂ tsp ground cumin

¹/₂ tsp ground coriander

1 cooked Tandoori Chicken (see page 156), cut into 8 pieces

4 tbsp heavy cream

to garnish

4 tbsp cashew nuts, lightly toasted and chopped

fresh cilantro sprigs

1 Put the onion and garlic and ginger paste in a food processor, blender, or spice grinder and whiz together until a paste forms. Add the tomatoes, chili powder, the sugar, and a pinch of salt and whiz again until blended.

2 Melt the ghee in a kadhai, wok, or large skillet over medium-high heat. Add the tomato mixture and water, stirring in the tomato paste.

3 Bring the mixture to a boil, stirring, then reduce the heat to very low and simmer for 5 minutes, stirring occasionally, until the sauce thickens.

4 Stir in half the butter, the garam masala, cumin, and coriander. Add the chicken pieces and stir around until they are well coated. Simmer for about an additional 10 minutes, or until the chicken is hot. Taste and adjust the seasoning, if necessary.

5 Lightly beat the cream in a small bowl and stir in several tablespoons of the hot sauce, beating constantly. Stir the cream mixture into the tomato sauce, then add the remaining butter and stir until it melts. Garnish with the chopped cashew nuts and cilantro sprigs and serve straight from the pan.

160 quick chicken curry with mushrooms and beans
murgh mushroom rasedaar

A quick-and-easy, rich curry that takes less time to prepare than more traditional Indian dishes.

SERVES 4–6

4 tbsp Ghee (see page 253) or vegetable or peanut oil

8 skinless, boneless chicken thighs, sliced

1 small onion, chopped

2 large garlic cloves, crushed

3½ oz/100 g green beans, trimmed and chopped

3½ oz/100 g mushrooms, thickly sliced

2 tbsp milk

salt and pepper

fresh cilantro sprigs, to garnish

for the curry paste

2 tsp Garam Masala (see page 251)

1 tsp mild, medium, or hot curry powder, to taste

1 tbsp water

1 To make the curry paste, put the garam masala and curry powder in a bowl and stir in the water, then set aside.

2 Melt half the ghee in a large, heavy-bottom pan or skillet with a tight-fitting lid over medium-high heat. Add the chicken pieces and curry paste and stir around for 5 minutes.

3 Add the onion, garlic, and green beans and continue cooking for an additional 5 minutes until the chicken is cooked through and the juices run clear when pierced with the tip of a knife.

4 Add the remaining ghee and mushrooms and, when the ghee melts, stir in the milk. Season to taste with salt and pepper. Reduce the heat to low, cover, and simmer for 10 minutes, stirring occasionally.

chicken tikka masala
murgh tikka makhani

This Indian dish reputedly started life in London restaurants as a way to use up leftover cooked tandoori chicken. It has now gone full cycle and is prepared in Indian restaurants. The quickest way to make this is to buy cooked tandoori chicken pieces from a supermarket or an Indian takeout. If, however, you want to make your own tandoori chicken, follow the recipe on page 156, then cut the cooked bird into pieces.

SERVES 4–6

14 oz/400 g canned chopped tomatoes

1¼ cups heavy cream

8 pieces cooked tandoori chicken (see page 156)

fresh cilantro sprigs, to garnish

for the tikka masala

2 tbsp Ghee (see page 253) or vegetable or peanut oil

1 large garlic clove, finely chopped

1 fresh red chili, seeded and chopped

2 tsp ground cumin

2 tsp ground paprika

½ tsp salt

pepper

1 To make the tikka masala, melt the ghee in a large skillet with a lid over medium heat. Add the garlic and chili and stir-fry for 1 minute. Stir in the cumin, paprika, salt, and pepper to taste and continue stirring for about 30 seconds.

2 Stir the tomatoes with their juice and the cream into the pan. Reduce the heat to low and let the sauce simmer for about 10 minutes, stirring frequently, until it reduces and thickens.

3 Meanwhile, remove all the bones and any skin from the tandoori chicken pieces, then cut the meat into bite-size pieces.

4 Adjust the seasoning of the sauce, if necessary. Add the chicken pieces to the pan, cover, and let simmer for 3–5 minutes until the chicken is heated through. Sprinkle with the cilantro sprigs.

162

kashmiri chicken
murgh kashmiri

This mild and aromatic Kashmiri dish is delicately flavored and colored with saffron threads, grown in the northern region. Chicken thighs are used in this recipe, but any pieces of boneless meat are suitable.

SERVES 4–6

seeds from 8 green cardamom pods

¹/₂ tsp coriander seeds

¹/₂ tsp cumin seeds

1 cinnamon stick

8 black peppercorns

6 cloves

1 tbsp hot water

¹/₂ tsp saffron threads

3 tbsp Ghee (see page 253) or vegetable or peanut oil

1 large onion, finely chopped

2 tbsp Garlic and Ginger Paste (see page 27)

generous 1 cup plain yogurt

8 skinless, boneless chicken thighs, sliced

3 tbsp ground almonds

generous ¹/₃ cup blanched pistachios, finely chopped

2 tbsp chopped fresh cilantro

2 tbsp chopped fresh mint*

salt

toasted slivered almonds, to garnish

1 Dry-roast the cardamom seeds in a hot skillet over medium-low heat, stirring constantly, until you can smell the aroma. Immediately tip them out of the pan so they don't burn. Repeat with the coriander and cumin seeds, cinnamon stick, peppercorns, and cloves. Put all the spices, except the cinnamon stick, in a spice grinder, or use a pestle and mortar, and grind to a powder.

2 Put the water and saffron threads in a small bowl and set aside.

3 Melt the ghee in a flameproof casserole or large skillet with a tight-fitting lid over medium-high heat. Add the onion and sauté, stirring occasionally, for 5–8 minutes until it becomes golden brown. Add the garlic and ginger paste and continue stirring for 2 minutes.

4 Stir in the ground spices* and the cinnamon stick. Take the onion mixture off the heat and mix in the yogurt, a small amount at a time, stirring vigorously with each addition, then return to the heat and continue stirring for 2–3 minutes until the ghee separates. Add the chicken pieces.

5 Bring the mixture to a boil, stirring constantly, then reduce the heat to the lowest setting, cover the pan, and simmer for 20 minutes, stirring occasionally and checking that the mixture isn't catching on the bottom of the pan. If it does start to catch, stir in a few tablespoons of water.

6 Stir the ground almonds, pistachios, saffron liquid, half the cilantro, all the mint leaves, and salt to taste into the chicken. Re-cover the pan and continue simmering for about 5 minutes until the chicken is tender and the sauce is thickened. Sprinkle with the remaining cilantro and slivered almonds.

*cook's tips

The mint leaves add a wonderful aroma to the dish
in Step 6 but, unfortunately, the heat turns them an
unappetizing dark color. That is why extra cilantro is
sprinkled over the dish just before serving. This rich dish
is very mild, making it ideal for anyone new to Indian
food who is worried about the food being too spicy.
However, $1/4$–$1/2$ teaspoon chili powder can be added with
the other ground spices in Step 4 for anyone who likes
more heat.

chicken jalfrezi
murgh jalfrezi

A "jalfrezi" is a wonderful hot curry cooked with fresh green chillies in a tomato, onion and pepper sauce. The sauce is also often used to make a vegetarian dish—just replace the chicken with firm, seasonal vegetables.

SERVES 4–6

4 tbsp Ghee (see page 253) or vegetable or peanut oil

8 skinless, boneless chicken thighs, sliced

1 large onion, chopped

2 tbsp Garlic and Ginger Paste (see page 27)

2 green bell peppers, cored, seeded, and chopped

1 large fresh green chili, seeded and finely chopped

1 tsp ground cumin

1 tsp ground coriander

$^1/_4$–$^1/_2$ tsp chili powder

$^1/_2$ tsp ground turmeric

$^1/_4$ tsp salt

14 oz/400 g canned chopped tomatoes

$^1/_2$ cup water

chopped fresh cilantro, to garnish

1 Melt half the ghee in a kadhai, wok, or large skillet over medium-high heat. Add the chicken pieces and stir around for 5 minutes until browned, but not necessarily cooked through, then remove from the pan with a slotted spoon and set aside.

2 Melt the remaining ghee in the pan. Add the onion and sauté, stirring frequently, for 5–8 minutes until golden brown. Stir in the garlic and ginger paste and continue sautéing for 2 minutes, stirring frequently.

3 Add the green bell peppers to the pan and stir around for 2 minutes.

4 Stir in the chilli, cumin, coriander, chili powder, turmeric, and salt. Add the tomatoes with their juice and the water* and bring to a boil.

5 Reduce the heat to low, add the chicken, and let simmer, uncovered, for 10 minutes, stirring frequently, until the bell peppers are tender, the chicken is cooked through, and the juices run clear if you pierce a few pieces with the tip of a knife. Sprinkle with the cilantro.

*cook's tip

To make this into a more filling meal that doesn't need any accompanying rice, add 14 oz/400 g chopped new potatoes with the tomatoes and water in Step 4. Bring to a boil, then reduce the heat and simmer for 5 minutes before you add the chicken.

SEAFOOD DISHES

Mumbai's bustling Sassoon Docks is actually one of India's largest fish markets, and each morning it is possible to see some of the bounty yielded from more than 3,700 kilometres of coastline, along with the catch from inland rivers, reservoirs, lakes, and southern backwaters.

Fishermen bring their catch on land for sale on the spot, for transporting around India, or for quick freezing before international shipping. It's a dazzling display that includes everything from huge tuna and sharks to tiny whitebait and shrimp, mussels and clams. Not necessarily for the faint-hearted, shimmering colors and blood and guts set the scene for hundreds of thousands of rupees to change hands, as restaurateurs, wholesalers, and home cooks look for the freshest and best bargains.

Bengal in the east and Goa and Kerala along the western Malabar coast are particularly known for their fresh seafood preparations, but, as in all aspects of Indian cooking, each region has its preferred style of flavoring and cooking. Fresh coconut flavors many dishes from Goa and Kerala, while mustard oil and mustard seeds are often used along with coconut in Bengal.

Bengalis, considered India's best seafood cooks, think nothing of eating fish and rice once or twice a day. Butterfish in Chili Yogurt (see page 189) is an example of the popular dishes served in Kolkata, where the colorful Bag Bazaar Market provides the city's cooks with fresh seafood. Fish Pakoras (see page 190), deep-fried in a light chickpea flour batter, are a tasty *chaat* cooked at the snack bars around the market. Serve with Cilantro Chutney (see page 245) to go with pre-dinner drinks. For a really quick-and-easy recipe that is equally good served hot or at room temperature, Pickled Mackerel (see page 186) with sautéed whole seeds is difficult to beat.

The photogenic ancient Chinese fishing nets of Fort Kochi are an icon in Kerala and have been bringing in the daily catch for more than 600 years, as well as a daily pull of tourists today. It's almost impossible to eat fresher seafood than at the numerous eating shacks situated alongside the fishing nets. The just-caught fish is displayed for selection, then cooked and flavored to order. Mussels with Mustard Seeds and Shallots (see page 177), which is equally delicious made with the large local shrimp, could be one of the quickly cooked dishes.

For Kerala's fishermen, who set out in the middle of the night, breakfast or lunch may well be a *molee*, the region's most popular fish stew flavored with coconut. It will be cooked on board with whatever fish the day's catch has provided. Nothing is wasted and heads and tails go into the pot, along with coconut milk and spices. The final dish can be very hot or mild, all depending on the cook's preference. For a slightly more refined mixed seafood curry, try the Goan-style Seafood Curry (see page 182) with a mixture of shrimp and white fish in a creamy, spiced coconut broth, colored with vibrant turmeric.

Any visit to tranquil Goa has to include sampling the fresh fish dishes that are cooked all day and late into the night at the numerous open-air beach shacks. Shrimp, mussels, butterfish, crabs, and lobsters are among the variety cooked to order.

Fishermen's wives are often in charge of sorting and selling the day's catch

170

For a taste of the Malabar coast, try butterfish

Indian cooks, especially in the coastal communities, have many recipes for cooking individual portions of fish wrapped in banana leaves, and the aromatic steamed version on page 178 comes from Mumbai's Parsi community. Each piece of fish is smeared with fresh cilantro chutney before it is wrapped to provide the most wonderful aromas when the pockets are opened at the table.

As Indian restaurants have proliferated outside the country, the availability of specific fish from Indian waters has followed. Many specimens are now sold frozen at supermarkets. For a taste of the Malabar coast, try butterfish, a delicately flavored white fish that is popular on the subcontinent. It tastes similar to sole, and can be broiled, pan-fried, or baked. Other particular Indian specialties to look for include pearlspot, also from the Malabar coast, and goat fish, with a shimmering rosy red skin.

As anyone who has ever ordered Bombay duck in an Indian or Chinese restaurant knows, it has never had webbed feet or a flat bill. It's actually a small, translucent fish that is salted and hung to dry in the hot Mumbai sun. It is then sold mostly as a snack, or to be crumbled and sprinkled over other dishes for extra flavor.

As with all fish recipes from anywhere in the world, Indian recipes rely on ultra-fresh seafood. Fish should never smell of anything other than a slight hint of the sea, the eyes should be clear, and the gills bright red. Any frozen fish should be cooked on the day it is thawed.

Right *Fresh swordfish can be bought on the beach*

Overleaf *Fishermen haul in their fishing nets on one of Goa's sandy beaches*

174

tandoori shrimp
tandoori jhinga

Quick and easy, this is one of the ways large jumbo shrimp are cooked in ramshackle-looking beach shacks along the Goan coast. Locals and tourists alike stroll along the sandy beaches and stop for just-cooked fish and shellfish served the way it always should be: ultra-fresh and simply cooked.

SERVES 4

4 tbsp plain yogurt

2 fresh green chilies, seeded and chopped

1/2 tbsp Garlic and Ginger Paste (see page 27)

seeds from 4 green cardamom pods

2 tsp ground cumin

1 tsp tomato paste

1/4 tsp ground turmeric

1/4 tsp salt

pinch of chili powder, ideally Kashmiri chili powder

24 raw jumbo shrimp, thawed if frozen, shelled, deveined, and tails left intact

lemon or lime wedges, to serve

1 Put the yogurt, chilies, and garlic and ginger paste in a small food processor or spice grinder and whiz until a paste forms. Alternatively use a pestle and mortar. Transfer the paste to a large nonmetallic bowl and stir in the cardamom seeds, cumin, tomato paste, turmeric, salt, and chili powder*.

2 Add the shrimp to the bowl and use your hands to make sure they are coated with the yogurt marinade. Cover the bowl with plastic wrap and chill for at least 30 minutes, or up to 4 hours.

3 When you are ready to cook, heat a large flat tava, griddle, or skillet over high heat until a few drops of water "dance" when they hit the surface. Use crumpled paper towels or a pastry brush to grease the hot pan very lightly with oil.

4 Use tongs to lift the shrimp out of the marinade, letting the excess drip back into the bowl, then place the shrimp on the tava and let them cook for 2 minutes. Flip the shrimp over and cook for an additional 1–2 minutes until they turn pink, curl, and are opaque all the way through when you cut one. Serve the shrimp at once with lemon or lime wedges for squeezing over.

*cook's tip

The spiced yogurt mixture also makes an excellent marinade for tandoori seafood kabobs. Cut 1 lb 10 oz/ 750 g thick, meaty fillets of white fish, such as cod, halibut, or angler fish, into 1 1/2-inch/4-cm cubes and put in the marinade with 12 or 16 large shelled and deveined shrimp. Let marinate for at least 30 minutes or up to 4 hours. When ready to cook, preheat the broiler to medium-high or light barbecue coals and leave until they turn gray. Thread the fish and shrimp on to 6 long, flat, greased metal skewers, alternating with pieces of blanched red or green bell peppers and/or white mushrooms. Broil for about 15 minutes, turning the skewers and brushing with any leftover marinade frequently, until the fish flakes and the edges of the fish are lightly charred.

mussels with mustard seeds and shallots   177
tissario kadugu

Baskets piled high with fresh mussels are not an uncommon slight along India's southern Malabar coast. Quickly cooked, fragrant dishes colored with golden turmeric like this are served in the open-air restaurants along Kochi's harborside, opposite the picturesque Chinese fishing nets.

SERVES 4

4 lb 8 oz/2 kg live mussels in their shells

3 tbsp vegetable or peanut oil

¹/₂ tbsp black mustard seeds

8 shallots, chopped

2 garlic cloves, crushed

2 tbsp distilled vinegar

4 small fresh red chilies

3 oz/85 g creamed coconut, dissolved in
  1 ¹/₄ cups boiling water

10 fresh curry leaves or 1 tbsp dried

¹/₂ tsp ground turmeric

¹/₄–¹/₂ tsp chili powder

salt

1 Pick over the mussels and discard any with broken shells or any open ones that do not close when firmly tapped. Scrub the mussels under cold running water to remove any barnacles and use a small knife to remove the "beards," if necessary, then set aside.

2 Heat the oil in a kadhai, wok, or large skillet over medium-high heat. Add the mustard seeds and stir them around for about 1 minute, or until they start to jump.

3 Add the shallots and garlic and sauté, stirring frequently, for 3 minutes, or until they start to brown. Stir in the vinegar, whole chilies, dissolved coconut, the curry leaves, turmeric, chili powder, and a pinch of salt and bring to a boil, stirring.

4 Reduce the heat to very low. Add the mussels, cover the pan, and let the mussels simmer, shaking the pan frequently, for 3–4 minutes, or until they are all open. Discard any that remain closed. Ladle the mussels into deep bowls, then taste the broth* and add extra salt, if necessary. Spoon over the mussels and serve.

*cook's tip
Taste the bright yellow broth before you add it to the mussels in Step 4. If the mussels were gritty, strain the liquid through a strainer lined with cheesecloth or paper towels. Mussels should be cooked on the day of purchase. When raw mussels don't close or cooked ones don't open, it is an indication that they aren't fresh or are dead. They must not be eaten.

178 steamed fish with cilantro chutney
paatrani machchi

Kerala's numerous tranquil backwaters are lined with elegant coconut trees, and the large leaves are often used in cooking or as a serving plate. Here, the glossy green leaves are wrapped around fresh fish fillets with a fresh-tasting chutney to keep the fish moist while it cooks. When these pockets are opened at the table, the vibrant flavors of southern India are unmistakable.

SERVES 4

1 quantity Cilantro Chutney (see page 245)

1 large fresh banana leaf*

vegetable or peanut oil

4 white fish fillets, such as butterfish or sole, about
  5 oz/140 g each

salt and pepper

lime or lemon wedges, to serve

1 Prepare the cilantro chutney recipe at least 2 hours in advance to allow the flavors to blend.

2 Meanwhile, cut the banana leaf into 4 squares that are large enough to fold comfortably around the fish to make tight pockets, about 10 inches/25 cm square.

3 Working with one piece of leaf at a time, very lightly rub the bottom with oil. Put one of the fish fillets in the center of the oiled side, flesh-side up. Spread one fourth of the cilantro chutney over the top and season to taste with salt and pepper.

4 Fold one side of the leaf over the fish, then fold the opposite side over. Turn the leaf so the folded edges are top and bottom. Fold the right-hand end of the leaf pocket into the center, then fold over the left-hand side. Trim the ends if the pocket becomes too bulky.

5 Use 2 wooden skewers to close the leaf pocket. Repeat with the remaining ingredients and banana leaf squares. The fish pockets can now be refrigerated for several hours.

6 When you are ready to cook the fish, place a steamer large enough to hold the pockets in a single layer over a pan of boiling water, without letting the water touch the fish. Add the fish, cover the pan, and steam for 15 minutes. Test by opening 1 pocket to make sure the fish is cooked through and flakes easily.

7 Serve the wrapped pockets with lime or lemon wedges and allow each guest to open their own to release the wonderful aromas.

*cook's tip

Fresh banana leaves are sold in the chilled cabinet of many Asian food stores. One large one should be sufficient for the 4 squares needed for this recipe, but it might be necessary to buy 2. If you can't find banana leaves, use foil, shiny-side up. Just take care to seal the edges tightly so none of the fragrant juices seep out.

The banana-leaf squares will be easier to fold if they are briefly dipped in a bowl of very hot water until they feel pliable. The banana leaves should be completely dried, however, before you add the oil in Step 3.

balti fish curry
machchli masala

This is for those who prefer robustly flavored dishes, more like the ones served in northern India, than the coconut-based ones from the south.

SERVES 4–6

2 lb/900 g thick fish fillets, such as angler fish, cod, or haddock, rinsed and cut into large chunks

2 bay leaves, torn

5 oz/140 g Ghee (see page 253) or ²/₃ cup vegetable or peanut oil

2 large onions, chopped

¹/₂ tbsp salt

²/₃ cup water

chopped fresh cilantro, to garnish

for the marinade

¹/₂ tbsp Garlic and Ginger Paste (see page 27)

1 fresh green chili, seeded and chopped

1 tsp ground coriander

1 tsp ground cumin

¹/₂ tsp ground turmeric

¹/₄–¹/₂ tsp chili powder

salt

1 tbsp water

1 To make the marinade, mix the garlic and ginger paste, green chili, coriander, cumin, turmeric, and chili powder together with salt to taste in a large bowl. Gradually stir in the water to form a thin paste. Add the fish chunks and smear with the marinade. Tuck the bay leaves underneath, cover, and let marinate in the refrigerator for at least 30 minutes, or up to 4 hours.

2 When you are ready to cook the fish, remove from the refrigerator 15 minutes in advance. Melt the ghee in a kadhai, wok, or large skillet over medium-high heat. Add the onions, sprinkle with the salt, and sauté, stirring frequently, for 8 minutes, or until they are very soft and golden*.

3 Gently add the fish and bay leaves to the pan and stir in the water. Bring to a boil, then immediately reduce the heat and cook the fish for 4–5 minutes, spooning the sauce over the fish and carefully moving the chunks around, until they are cooked through and the flesh flakes easily. Adjust the seasoning, if necessary, and sprinkle with cilantro.

*cook's tip
Do not over-brown the onions in Step 2 or the dish will taste bitter. They should be golden, but not brown, when the fish is added.

182

goan-style seafood curry
goa che nalla chi kadi

With mustard seeds, curry leaves, and a creamy coconut sauce, this quick-and-easy dish could easily have originated anywhere in southern India, not just in tropical Goa on the west coast. But it is in Goa that the coconut is king: the flesh and milk are used in sweet and savory dishes, and the carved shells are popular tourist souvenirs.

SERVES 4–6

3 tbsp vegetable or peanut oil

1 tbsp black mustard seeds

12 fresh curry leaves or 1 tbsp dried

6 shallots, finely chopped*

1 garlic clove, crushed

1 tsp ground turmeric

$^{1}/_{2}$ ground coriander

$^{1}/_{4}$–$^{1}/_{2}$ tsp chili powder

5 oz/140 g creamed coconut, grated and dissolved in
 1$^{1}/_{4}$ cups boiling water

1 lb 2 oz/500 g skinless, boneless white fish, such
 as angler fish or cod, cut into large chunks

1 lb/450 g large raw shrimp, shelled and deveined

juice and finely grated rind of 1 lime

salt

lime wedges, to serve

1 Heat the oil in a kadhai, wok, or large skillet over high heat. Add the mustard seeds and stir them around for about 1 minute, or until they jump. Stir in the curry leaves.

2 Add the shallots and garlic and stir for about 5 minutes, or until the shallots are golden. Stir in the turmeric, coriander, and chili powder and continue stirring for about 30 seconds.

3 Add the dissolved creamed coconut. Bring to a boil, then reduce the heat to medium and stir for about 2 minutes.

4 Reduce the heat to low, add the fish, and simmer for 1 minute, stirring the sauce over the fish and very gently stirring it around. Add the shrimp and continue to simmer for an additional 4–5 minutes until the fish flesh flakes easily and the shrimp turn pink and curl.

5 Add half the lime juice, then taste and add more lime juice and salt to taste. Sprinkle with the lime rind and serve with lime wedges.

*cook's tip

Peeling a large number of shallots like this can be time-consuming but the job is quicker if you submerge them in a pan of boiling water for 30–45 seconds. Drain the shallots and use a knife to slice off the root end, then they should peel easily.

shrimp pooris
jhinga puri

This restaurant favorite is easy to re-create at home. The deep-fried Pooris aren't difficult to make, but remember to leave enough time for the dough to rest for 20 minutes before it is cooked. Serve this as an appetizer or entrée, or make mini Pooris and serve the shrimp mixture as a dip.

SERVES 6

2 tsp coriander seeds

1/2 tsp black peppercorns

1 large garlic clove, crushed

1 tsp ground turmeric

1/4–1/2 tsp chili powder

1/2 tsp salt

3 tbsp Ghee (see page 253) or vegetable or peanut oil

1 onion, grated

1 lb 12 oz/800 g canned crushed tomatoes

pinch of sugar

1 lb 2 oz/500 g small cooked shelled shrimp, thawed if frozen

1/2 tsp Garam Masala (see page 251), plus extra to garnish

1/2 quantity Pooris* (see page 240), kept warm

fresh cilantro, to garnish

1 Put the coriander seeds, peppercorns, garlic, turmeric, chili powder, and salt in a small food processor or spice grinder, or use a pestle and mortar, and blend to a thick paste.

2 Melt the ghee in a kadhai, wok, or large skillet over medium-low heat. Add the paste and cook, stirring constantly, for about 30 seconds.

3 Add the grated onion and stir around for an additional 30 seconds. Stir in the tomatoes and their juice and the sugar. Bring to a boil, stirring, and let bubble for 10 minutes, mashing the tomatoes against the side of the pan to break them down, or until reduced. Taste and add extra salt, if necessary.

4 Add the shrimp and sprinkle with the garam masala. When the shrimp are hot, arrange the hot pooris on plates and top each one with a portion of the shrimp. Sprinkle with the cilantro and garam masala.

*cook's tip

Deep-fried pooris are best served straight from the pan, so it is a good idea to have a couple of pans to use if you are entertaining. The pooris, with their rich, light texture, are traditional with this dish, but chapatis or naans are also good, especially if you want to avoid last-minute deep-frying.

186

pickled mackerel
bhangde lonchen

This quick and crunchy dish is equally good served hot, straight from the pan, or when cooled to room temperature.

SERVES 4

vegetable or peanut oil

finely grated rind and juice of 1 lime

salt and pepper

4 large mackerel fillets, about 6 oz/175 g each*

1¹/₂ tsp cumin seeds

1¹/₂ tsp black mustard seeds

1¹/₂ tsp nigella seeds

1¹/₂ tsp fennel seeds

1¹/₂ tsp coriander seeds

1¹/₂-inch/4-cm piece fresh gingerroot,
   very finely chopped

1¹/₂ garlic cloves, very finely chopped

3 shallots, very finely chopped

pinch of chili powder

fresh red chilies, seeded and very finely sliced, to garnish

lime wedges, to serve

1 Mix together 2 tablespoons of oil, the lime rind and juice, and salt and pepper to taste in a nonmetallic bowl that will hold the mackerel fillets in a flat layer. Add the mackerel fillets and use your hands to cover them in the marinade, then set aside for at least 10 minutes, or cover and chill for up to 4 hours.

2 Meanwhile, preheat the broiler to high, and lightly brush the broiler with oil.

3 Remove the mackerel from the refrigerator 15 minutes in advance. Put the mackerel on the broiler, skin-side down, and broil about 4 inches/10 cm from the source of the heat for 6 minutes, or until the flesh is cooked through when pierced with the tip of a knife and flakes easily.

4 While the mackerel broils, heat 2 tablespoons of oil in a kadhai, wok, or large skillet over medium-high heat. Add the cumin, black mustard, nigella, fennel, and coriander seeds and stir around until the black mustard seeds start to jump and the coriander and cumin seeds just start to brown. Immediately remove the pan from the heat and stir in the ginger, garlic, shallots, and chili powder and continue stirring for 1 minute.

5 Transfer the mackerel fillets to plates and spoon the spice mixture over. Garnish with red chili slices and serve with lime wedges for squeezing over.

*cook's tip
The spicy flavor of this recipe works well with any oily fish fillets, so try herring, salmon, and tuna as well.

butterfish in chili yogurt
dahi pamplet

Seafood is an important part of the everyday Bengali diet, where this dish using butterfish fillets originates. Butterfish, with its excellent flavor and delicate texture, is one of the jewels of Indian seafood cooking. If you cannot find butterfish, flounder or sole can be substituted.

SERVES 4

2 tbsp vegetable or peanut oil

1 large onion, sliced

1¹/₂-inch/4-cm piece fresh gingerroot,
   finely chopped

¹/₂ tsp salt

¹/₄ tsp ground turmeric

pinch of ground cinnamon

pinch of ground cloves

generous ¹/₄ cup plain yogurt

1 tbsp all-purpose flour

small pinch of chili powder

salt and pepper

4 skinless butterfish fillets, about 5¹/₂ oz/150 g each,
   wiped dry

2 tbsp Ghee (see page 253) or vegetable or peanut oil

2 fresh fat green chilies, seeded and finely chopped

1 Heat the oil in a large skillet over medium-high heat. Add the onion and sauté, stirring, for 8 minutes, or until it is soft and dark golden brown. Add the ginger and stir around for an additional minute.

2 Stir in the salt, turmeric, cinnamon, and cloves and continue stirring for 30 seconds. Remove the pan from the heat and stir in the yogurt, a little at a time, beating constantly.

3 Transfer the yogurt mixture to a food processor or blender and whiz until a paste forms.

4 Season the flour with chili powder and salt and pepper to taste. Place it on a plate and lightly dust the fish fillets on both sides.

5 Melt the ghee in the wiped pan over medium-high heat. When it is bubbling, turn the heat to medium and add the fillets in a single layer. Pan-fry for 2¹/₂ minutes, or until golden, then turn them over.

6 Continue cooking for an additional minute, then return the yogurt sauce to the pan and reheat, stirring. When the fillets flake easily and are cooked through and the sauce is hot, transfer to plates and sprinkle with the chili.

Indian seafood is fished from rivers and backwaters, as well as the west and east coasts

fish pakoras
machchli pakora

After a morning's stroll through the ancient town of Kochi in Kerala, simple, cooked-to-order pakoras like these make a relaxing lunch by the harborside fish market. These are ideal for a quick family meal or as a snack to enjoy with drinks.

SERVES 4–6

¹/₂ tsp salt

2 tbsp lemon juice or distilled white vinegar

pepper

1 lb 9 oz/700 g skinless white fish fillets, such as cod, halibut, or angler fish, rinsed, patted dry, and cut into large chunks

vegetable or peanut oil, for deep-frying

lemon wedges, to serve

for the batter

1 cup besan or gram flour

seeds from 4 green cardamom pods

large pinch of ground turmeric

large pinch of baking soda

finely grated rind of 1 lemon

salt and pepper

³/₄ cup water

1 Combine the salt, lemon juice, and pepper to taste and rub all over the fish chunks, then set aside in a nonmetallic bowl and let stand for 20–30 minutes.

2 Meanwhile, to make the batter*, put the besan flour in a bowl and stir in the seeds from the cardamom pods, turmeric, baking soda, lemon rind, and salt and pepper to taste. Make a well in the center and gradually stir in the water until a thin batter similar to light cream forms.

3 Gently stir the pieces of fish into the batter, taking care not to break them up.

4 Heat enough oil for deep-frying in a kadhai, wok, deep-fat fryer, or large, heavy-bottom pan to 350°F/180°C, or until a cube of bread browns in 30 seconds. Remove the fish pieces from the batter and let the excess batter drip back into the bowl. Without overcrowding the pan, drop fish pieces in the hot fat and cook for about 2¹/₂–3 minutes until golden brown.

5 Immediately use a slotted spoon to remove the fish pieces from the fat and drain on crumpled paper towels. Continue until all the fish is cooked, then serve hot with the lemon wedges.

* cook's tip

The batter can be made several hours in advance and set aside covered with plastic wrap. Stir it well before using, and add a little extra water if it has become too thick. If the batter is too thick it will remain raw next to the fish.

DESSERTS
& DRINKS

194 It is somewhat ironic that Indians are known around the world for their love of sweet food, yet don't eat desserts on a daily basis. Instead, family meals are more likely to end with a plate of prepared fresh fruits, selected for their seasonal availability. What Indians do find irresistible, however, is the colorful and appealing display of sweetmeats sold in the numerous *mithai*, candy stores, especially in the crowded cities.

Bengalis are known for their sweetmeat preparations, and congregating at *mithai* shops is a part of daily life in Kolkata. Decorating the sweetmeats with ultra-thin flecks of silver called *varak* only adds to the dazzling window displays.

When it comes to weddings, birthdays, religious celebrations, and other special occasions, sweet desserts will be plentiful. The best-known Indian desserts are rich with dairy products or cooked in ghee and a small amount often suffices.

At first glance, some of the most popular Indian desserts appear similar to their Western counterparts, but when you read the recipes it becomes clear these are uniquely Indian. From northern India, Kheer (see page 200), the traditional rice dessert, is flavored with cardamom, topped with nuts, and occasionally silver *varak*, a reflection of the days it was served at Moghul banquets. Indian Kheer, slowly simmered on the stove, is much sweeter and richer than rice desserts in Europe or America. This dessert is often part of Hindu feasts, as the god Rama is said to have been conceived after his mother ate a divine portion of Kheer.

Whereas European bread puddings are everyday desserts for family meals, *shahi tukda*, the Indian Bread Pudding (see page 206), is cooked in ghee and flavored and colored with cardamom and saffron, a legacy from the days it was served in Moghul courts. It is too rich to eat except on special occasions.

European cooking has used the sweetness of carrots and parsnips to flavor desserts since medieval times, but nothing comes close to the rich and filling Carrot Halva (see page 203) from the Punjab and Gujarat. Flavored with cardamom and pistachios, this is a must at Hindu and Sikh weddings, when it is usually finished with a final *varak* decoration. It can be served hot or cold, with or without cream or ice cream. When made in Gujarat, the bright red-orange carrots that grow there give this dessert a deep, jewel-like color.

For a creamy, rich elegance, few desserts surpass the strained yogurt mixture of Shrikhand with Pomegranate (see page 207), the name of which translates as "ambrosia of the gods." The subtle flavoring of cardamom and saffron transforms this surprisingly economical dessert into something very special. In Maharashtra, Shrikhand is traditionally accompanied by just-cooked Pooris (see page 240), but it is also fantastic served with fresh tropical fruits, such as mango, passion fruit, melon, or even more everyday plantains or bananas.

Another economical Indian dessert that tastes rich and extravagant is Payasam (see page 201) from the south. Vermicelli noodles, like Italian angel hair pasta, are simmered in sweetened milk with nuts. During the month-long Muslim festival of Ramadan, this is often included in the feast that breaks the day's fast.

Kulfi, the Indian ice cream that is traditionally frozen in tall, cone-shaped molds, is a firm favorite with young and old alike everywhere in India. It's difficult to find anyone who doesn't devour this extra-sweet chilled dessert, but it isn't quite as easy to find anyone who actually makes it at home. Although not difficult, there isn't much point in India as stores and roadside stalls sell it in almost every flavor imaginable. Try the version flavored with almonds and saffron on page 204.

Alcoholic drinks are not a common part of Indian meals, except perhaps ice-cold Indian beer. Some states prohibit the sale of any alcohol, and when it is allowed, foreign wines and spirits are so heavily taxed that they become quite a luxury, even for tourists in

Left A candymaker at work on his stall in Mysore in the province of Karnataka

Overleaf Women in festive dress attend one of the many religious festivals celebrated both nationally and locally

It's difficult to find anyone who doesn't devour this extra-sweet chilled dessert

five-star hotels. Sparkling wine from Maharashtra, when available, goes surprisingly well with many spicy dishes. A more traditional option, however, is a glass of Salt Lassi (see page 212), the cooling yogurt and water drink that is like a raita in a glass. Mango Lassi (see page 213) is a refreshing version for a hot, sunny day, as is the sharp-tasting Ginger Cordial (see page 217), with a hint of lemon. Indians are great tea drinkers and Masala Tea (see page 214), flavored with whole spices, is an everyday favorite. Drink it black or with milk. In India it is always served hot, but chilled it is a real thirst-quencher. The Pistachio and Almond Shake (see page 216) is like a liquid form of Kulfi. It's rich and thick and best served in small glasses.

200 kheer
kheer

One of the most popular desserts in India, kheer appears on all restaurant menus and is rarely missing from wedding feasts or Hindu and Muslim religious festivals. This rich, creamy dessert from northern India can be served hot or chilled, thick or very liquid with the rice floating in the milk, or flavored with many different spices and fruits. Try this lightly spiced version chilled with fresh pineapple or mango slices for a treat.

SERVES 4–6

scant ¹/₂ cup basmati rice

1 quart milk

seeds from 4 green cardamom pods

1 cinnamon stick

¹/₂ cup superfine sugar, or to taste

to serve

grated jaggery or brown sugar (optional)

chopped toasted pistachios (optional)

1 Rinse the basmati rice in several changes of water until the water runs clear, then let soak for 30 minutes. Drain and set aside until ready to cook.

2 Rinse the pan with cold water and do not dry. Pour the milk into the pan, add the cardamom seeds and cinnamon stick, and stir in the rice and sugar.

3 Put the pan over medium-high heat and slowly bring to a boil, stirring. Reduce the heat to its lowest setting and let the mixture simmer, stirring frequently, for about 1 hour, until the rice is tender and the milky mixture has thickened. When the rice is tender you can stir in extra milk if you like the dessert with a soupier texture, or continue simmering if you like it thicker.

4 Spoon into individual bowls and sprinkle with jaggery to serve hot, or transfer to a bowl and let cool completely, stirring frequently. Cover and chill until ready to serve. Spoon the rice into individual bowls and sprinkle with the nuts*.

*cook's tip
Transform this into a celebration dessert by decorating it with silver leaf.

payasam
payasam

This classic Indian dessert is made from very fine wheat noodles called sevian.

SERVES 4–6

2 tbsp Ghee (see page 253) or vegetable or peanut oil

6 oz/175 g sevian or vermicelli noodles, broken into 3-inch/7.5-cm pieces

¼ cup almonds or cashew nuts

4 cups of milk

2 oz/55 g creamed coconut, crumbled

6 tbsp superfine sugar

2 tbsp raisins or golden raisins

pinch of salt

1 Melt the ghee in a kadhai, wok, or large pan* over medium heat. Add the sevian and stir for just 1–2 minutes until they turn a light golden brown. Use a slotted spoon to remove them from the pan and set aside.

2 Add the nuts to the pan and stir them around until they start to turn golden brown. Immediately stir in the milk, creamed coconut, sugar, raisins, and salt.

3 Return the noodles to the pan. Bring the milk to a boil, then reduce the heat and simmer, uncovered and stirring almost constantly, for about 30 minutes, or until the noodles are tender and the milk is reduced. Taste and add extra sugar, if desired.

*cook's tip

If you don't have a kadhai or wok, use the widest pan you have. The wider the pan, the quicker the milk will reduce. Be sure to use a heavy-bottom pan, otherwise the milk might catch on the bottom and burn.

carrot halva
gajar ka halwa

This is an example of the very sweet desserts most Indians adore. Originally from the Punjab and northern Indian, this rich, filling dessert can be served hot or chilled. In winter, it is often served hot with ice cream.

SERVES 4–6

3 cups milk

²/₃ cup light cream

1 lb 2 oz/500 g carrots, coarsely grated

scant ¹/₂ cup superfine sugar

1 tbsp brown sugar

4 tbsp Ghee (see page 253) or butter, melted

1 cup ground almonds

seeds of 6 green cardamom pods, lightly crushed

3 tbsp raisins or golden raisins

to decorate

blanched almonds, toasted and chopped

pistachios, chopped

silver leaf (optional)*

1 Rinse a large, heavy-bottom pan with cold water and do not dry. Pour the milk and cream into the pan, then stir in the carrots and put the pan over high heat. Slowly bring to a boil, stirring.

2 Reduce the heat to its lowest setting and simmer, stirring frequently, for 2 hours, or until most of the milk has evaporated and the carrots are thickened.

3 Stir in the superfine and brown sugars, then continue simmering for an additional 30 minutes, stirring almost constantly to prevent the mixture from catching on the bottom of the pan.

4 Stir in the ghee, ground almonds, cardamom seeds, and raisins. Continue simmering, stirring constantly, until the mixture is thick and there is a thin layer of ghee on the surface.

5 Stir the mixture well, then transfer to a serving dish. Sprinkle the surface with the nuts and add thin flecks of silver leaf, if you like.

*cook's tip

For an Indian wedding or other special occasion, the top of this dish will be decorated with the thinnest pieces of edible, pounded silver, called silver leaf or *varak*. It is sold in upmarket Indian food stores and is very easy to use. Each sheet of silver leaf has a paper backing. Put the silver side down on to the dessert, with the paper backing facing up, and use a paintbrush or pastry brush to dab on the paper. The silver will then transfer to the dessert. The trick is not to touch the silver with your fingers or it will stick.

Fruits and vegetables are very important parts of the Indian diet

204 # saffron and almond kulfi
kesar badaam kulfi

Kulfi, or Indian ice cream, comes in a seemingly unlimited variety of flavors—just about all fresh fruits, nuts, and spices are used. This version, flavored with golden saffron, reflects the creamy dessert's Moghul heritage and ancient manuscripts describe a similar dessert being prepared for Emperor Akbar's lavish feasts in the late sixteenth and early seventeenth centuries. When you are served kulfi in India, it will have been frozen in a tall, conical metal or plastic mold. These molds are sold at Indian cookware stores, but you can use freezerproof ramekins instead.

MAKES 4

½ tsp saffron threads

5 tbsp milk

1 tbsp ground rice

½ tbsp ground almonds

1 cup canned evaporated milk

1 cup heavy cream

2 tbsp superfine sugar

2 tbsp chopped toasted blanched almonds, to serve

1 Put the saffron threads in a dry skillet over high heat and "toast," stirring frequently until you can smell the aroma, then immediately tip them out of the pan.

2 Put the milk in the skillet over medium-high heat, add the saffron threads, and heat just until small bubbles appear around the edge. Remove the pan from the heat and let the saffron infuse for at least 15 minutes. Meanwhile, combine the ground rice and ground almonds in a heatproof bowl. Put a flat freezerproof container into the freezer.

3 Reheat the milk and saffron just until small bubbles appear around the edge, then slowly beat the milk into the almond mixture, beating until it is smooth without any lumps.

4 Pour the evaporated milk into a pan over medium-high heat and bring to a boil, stirring. Remove the pan from the heat and stir into the milk mixture. Stir in the cream and sugar.

5 Return the pan to medium heat and simmer, stirring constantly, for 5–10 minutes until it thickens, but do not boil. Remove the pan from the heat and set aside, stirring frequently, to cool.

6 Pour the saffron mixture into the freezerproof bowl and freeze for 30 minutes, then beat to break up any ice crystals. Continue beating every 30 minutes until the ice cream is thick and almost firm. If you are using metal kulfi molds, put them in the freezer now.

7 Equally divide the mixture among 4 kulfi molds or ramekins. Cover with the lid or plastic wrap and freeze for at least 2 hours until solid.

8 To serve, dip a dish towel in hot water, wring it out, and rub it around the sides of the molds or ramekins, then invert on to plates. Sprinkle with the toasted almonds and serve.

206

indian bread pudding
shahi tukda

From the tradition of lavish Moghul cooking in Hyderabad, this luscious bread pudding is flavored and colored with saffron.

SERVES 4–6

pinch of saffron threads

²/₃ cup heavy cream, plus extra to serve

²/₃ cup milk

generous ¹/₄ cup superfine sugar

seeds from 3 green cardamom pods

¹/₂ cinnamon stick

1¹/₂ oz/40 g dried mixed fruits, such as apricots, mangoes, and figs, finely chopped

3 oz/85 g Ghee (see page 253) or 6 tbsp vegetable or peanut oil

6 slices white bread, crusts removed and cut into triangles

freshly grated nutmeg, to garnish

1 Put the saffron threads in a dry pan over high heat and "toast," stirring frequently, until you can smell the aroma. Immediately tip them out of the pan.

2 Put the cream, milk, sugar, cardamom seeds, cinnamon stick, and fruits in the pan over medium-high heat. Add the saffron threads and heat just until small bubbles appear around the edge, stirring to dissolve the sugar. Remove the pan from the heat and let the saffron infuse for at least 15 minutes.

3 Meanwhile, preheat the oven to 400°F/200°C and lightly grease a 10 x 7-inch/25 x 18-cm ovenproof serving dish.

4 Melt a third of the ghee in a large skillet over medium-high heat. Add as many bread triangles as will fit in a single layer and pan-fry until golden brown, then turn over and repeat on the other side. Remove from the pan and drain on some crumpled paper towels. Continue pan-frying all the bread triangles, adding more ghee, as necessary.

5 Arrange the bread slices in the ovenproof dish and pour the cream and flavorings over, removing the cinnamon stick. Bake for 20 minutes, or until the top is golden brown. Let stand for a few minutes, then lightly grate fresh nutmeg over the top. Serve hot with chilled cream for pouring over.

The University and Rajbai Clock Tower overlooks the Oval Maidan Park in Mumbai

This is the western Indian way of transforming everyday plain yogurt into a luscious, creamy dessert. Any fruits can be used for the topping, but it is a chance to enjoy the most exotic you can find. This is traditionally served with hot Pooris (see page 240), straight from the pan, although it is satisfying served on its own.

shrikhand with pomegranate
shrikhand anaari

207

SERVES 4

4 cups plain yogurt

¹/₄ tsp saffron threads

2 tbsp milk

generous ¹/₄ cup superfine sugar, to taste

seeds of 2 green cardamom pods

2 pomegranates or other exotic fruits

1 Line a strainer set over a bowl with a piece of cheesecloth large enough to hang over the edge. Add the yogurt, then tie the corners of the cheesecloth into a tight knot and tie them to a faucet. Let the bundle hang over the sink for 4 hours, or until all the excess moisture drips away.

2 Put the saffron threads in a dry pan over high heat and "toast," stirring frequently, until you can smell the aroma. Immediately tip them out of the pan. Put the milk in the pan, return the saffron threads, and warm just until bubbles appear around the edge, then set aside and let infuse.

3 When the yogurt is thick and creamy, put it in a bowl, stir in the sugar, cardamom pods, and saffron-flavored milk, and beat until smooth. Taste and add extra sugar, if desired. Cover and chill for at least 1 hour until well chilled.

4 Meanwhile, to prepare the pomegranate seeds, cut the fruits in half and use a small teaspoon or your fingers to scoop out the seeds.

5 To serve, spoon the yogurt into individual bowls or plates and add the pomegranate seeds*.

*cook's tip
For a more everyday, family dessert, omit the saffron and cardamom seeds. Flavor the thickened yogurt with sugar and ground ginger and cinnamon to taste, or top with sliced bananas or oranges. The yogurt is also good flavored with vanilla seeds and extra sugar

Overleaf A woman sits overlooking the Ganges at Varanasi (Benares) in Uttar Pradesh Province

spiced fruit salad
phal ki chaat

Fresh fruits, simply prepared, are often a welcome, light alternative to the traditional sweet Indian desserts. This refreshing, mildly spiced salad can be made with any fruits, and the more variety you include, the better. It makes a particularly good ending to a spicy meal.

SERVES 4–6

finely grated rind and juice of 1 lime

1 lb/450 g fresh fruits, such as bananas, guavas, oranges, kumquats, mangoes, melons, and pineapple*

yogurt, to serve

for the spiced syrup

1¹/₄ cups superfine sugar

²/₃ cup water

1 vanilla bean, sliced lengthwise, but left whole

1 cinnamon stick, broken in half

¹/₂ tsp fennel seeds

¹/₂ tsp black peppercorns, lightly crushed

¹/₂ tsp cumin seeds

1 Begin by making the spiced syrup. Put the sugar, half the water, vanilla bean, cinnamon stick, fennel seeds, peppercorns, and cumin seeds into a small, heavy-bottom pan over medium-high heat. Slowly bring to a boil, stirring to dissolve the sugar. As soon as the sugar boils, stop stirring and let the syrup bubble until it turns a golden brown.

2 Stand back from the pan and stir in the remaining water: the syrup will splash and splatter. Stir again to dissolve any caramel, then remove the pan from the heat and let the syrup cool slightly.

3 Meanwhile, put the lime rind and juice in a large, heatproof bowl. Prepare and cut each fruit as required and add it to the bowl. If you are using bananas, toss them immediately in the lime juice to prevent discoloration.

4 Pour in the syrup and let the fruits and syrup cool completely, then cover the bowl and chill for at least 1 hour before serving with thick, creamy yogurt.

*cook's tip

If you are including oranges, pineapples, or any other juicy fruits, be sure to include the juice and squeeze the membranes and peels to extract extra juice. Work over the bowl when segmenting fruits to catch the juices.

salt lassi
namkeen lassi

"Salt lassi or sweet lassi?" This is the question anyone in India has to answer over and over. This chilled yogurt drink is universally popular and served everywhere, from the grandest hotels to the most humble beachside eating shacks. Many Indians drink lassi with meals, rather than beer or wine.

MAKES 4–6

3 cups plain yogurt

$\frac{1}{2}$ tsp salt

$\frac{1}{4}$ tsp sugar

generous 1 cup water

ice cubes

to garnish

ground cumin

fresh mint sprigs

1 Beat the yogurt, salt, and sugar together in a pitcher or bowl, then add the water and whisk until frothy.

2 Fill 4 to 6 glasses with ice cubes and pour the yogurt mixture over. Lightly dust the top of each glass with ground cumin and garnish with mint*.

*cook's tip

For a sweet lassi, add 4 tablespoons sugar and omit the salt. You can also add $\frac{1}{2}$–1 teaspoon rose water, if you like. Pour over ice cubes and sprinkle with ground cumin and very finely chopped toasted pistachios.

Water buffalo, used on farms all over India, here take a cooling dip

mango lassi
aam ki lassi

Cool and creamy, an ice-chilled mango lassi is unbeatable when temperatures are rising. For sweetness, many Indians say it is worth the effort of searching out an Alphonso mango, and to save time, you will find Alphonso mango pulp in cans in Indian food stores.

MAKES 4–6

1 large mango, ideally an Alphonso mango,
  coarsely chopped*
3 cups plain yogurt
generous 1 cup cold water
2 tbsp superfine sugar, or to taste
fresh lime juice, to taste
ice cubes
ground ginger, to decorate (optional)

1 Put 9 oz/250 g of the mango flesh in a food processor or blender with the yogurt and whiz until smooth (use any remaining mango for a fruit salad). Add the water and whiz again to blend.

2 The amount of sugar you will add depends on how sweet the mango is. Taste and stir in sugar to taste, then stir in the lime juice.

3 Fill 4 to 6 glasses with ice cubes and pour the mango mixture over. Lightly dust the top of each glass with ground ginger, if you like.

cook's tip

When buying fresh mangoes, look for an unblemished skin. A ripe mango will yield slightly when you squeeze it, and you can try to bring on an underripe fruit by placing it with an apple in a plastic bag with a few holes poked through. The larger the mango, the greater the fruit to pit ratio will be. Take care when you cut the mango, because mango juice can stain.

214 masala tea
masalewali chai

There is always time for a cup of tea, or chai, *in India. Every office has a* chai walla, *and vendors sell it freshly brewed on street corners and at railroad stations. This milky version is drunk from the north to the south.*

MAKES 4–6 CUPS

4 cups water

1-inch/2.5-cm piece fresh gingerroot, coarsely chopped

1 cinnamon stick

3 green cardamom pods, crushed

3 cloves

1½ tbsp Assam tea leaves

sugar, to taste

milk

1 Pour the water into a heavy-bottom pan over medium-high heat. Add the ginger, cinnamon stick, cardamom, and cloves and bring to a boil. Reduce the heat and simmer for 10 minutes.

2 Put the tea leaves in a teapot and pour over the water and spices. Stir and let infuse for 5 minutes*.

3 Strain the tea into teacups and add sugar and milk to taste.

*cook's tip
For iced masala tea, let the tea cool completely in Step 2, then strain into a pitcher and chill. Serve in tall glasses over ice cubes with sugar to taste and lemon or lime wedges for squeezing in.

Tea grows in India on the hills of Darjeeling, Assam, and the Nilgiris and the leaves are picked by hand

216

pistachio and almond shake
pista-badaam doodh

The abundance of pistachios and almonds in India means the combination is often included in both savory and sweet dishes. Here, the nuts are made into a thick, rich milk shake, which is served for celebrations such as birthdays. This takes time to cool, however, so make it in advance and keep it in the refrigerator until time to serve. Just be sure to stir well before pouring into glasses. This drink is so rich you will probably want to serve it in smaller glasses than for more familiar Western milk shakes.

MAKES 4–6 SMALL GLASSES

pinch of saffron threads

²/₃ cup ground almonds

generous ³/₄ cup pistachios, very finely chopped

3 tbsp hot water

1³/₄ cups condensed milk

pinch of salt

2–3 scoops ice cream

1 Put the saffron threads in a dry skillet over high heat and "toast," stirring, until you can smell the aroma. Immediately tip them out of the pan.

2 Put the ground almonds, pistachios, and saffron threads in a spice grinder or large mortar and grind until a fine powder forms. Add the water and continue grinding until a paste forms.

3 Transfer the paste to a food processor or blender and add the condensed milk and salt. Whiz until blended, then add the ice cream to make a milk shake*. Transfer to a pitcher and chill until very cold. Stir well and serve.

*cook's tip

This mixture is so rich it can be frozen and served like an ice cream. After all the ingredients are incorporated in Step 3, transfer the mixture to a freezerproof container and put in the freezer, beating every 30 minutes or so, until it is solid.

ginger cordial

adrak ka sherbet

This chilled drink has a biting, sharp flavor that is thirst quenching in hot weather, especially the steamy weeks before the monsoons. Ginger is one of the most ancient spices in India, and its medicinal properties are legendary. It is credited with soothing upset stomachs, and drinks like this are often sipped after a large meal as a digestive.

MAKES 4–6 GLASSES

2¹/₂ oz/70 g fresh gingerroot, very finely chopped

¹/₂ tbsp finely grated lemon rind

1 quart boiling water

2 tbsp fresh lemon juice, or to taste

4 tbsp superfine sugar, or to taste

lemon and fresh mint, to decorate

1 Put the ginger in a heatproof bowl with the lemon rind. Pour over the boiling water, stir, and let steep overnight.

2 Strain the liquid into a large pitcher. Stir in the lemon juice and sugar, stirring until the sugar dissolves. Taste and add extra lemon juice and sugar, if you like. Serve decorated with lemon and mint.

ACCOMPANIMENTS

As is the style throughout Asia, side dishes in Indian meals have much more of a starring role than in Western cuisines. Without the tradition of eating a succession of courses, all the components of an Indian meal, from soup through to dessert, are served at once.

Traditionally meals are served *thali*-style on a large, round plate in the north or on a banana leaf in the south. Individual portions of a meat, poultry, seafood, or a vegetarian dish are accompanied by rice and/or bread, a selection of fresh chutneys, and a creamy yogurt Raita (see page 244) and are served in small bowls called *katoris* around the *thali*. It is the rice dishes, breads, and chutneys, which would be considered mere accompaniments in the West, that make Indian dining such an exciting feast of colors and tastes.

Regardless of whether the meal is "veg" or "non-veg," it always includes a starch in the form of rice or bread or both. Indian *roti*, or breads, not only have a nutritional role, but also replace knives and forks, as most Indians eat with their fingers. The malleable texture of unleavened Chapatis (see page 236) and ghee-rich flaky Parathas (see page 239) make it easy to use a torn piece of bread to scoop up bite-size portions of food. Both these breads are quickly cooked on flat griddles, eliminating the need for an oven, which many basic Indian kitchens don't include. Large, lightly leavened Naans (see page 235), on the other hand, are quickly baked on the inside of *tandoor* ovens, which means these are usually bought at food stalls or in restaurants.

The wheat-based breads of the north are served to a lesser extent in the south. There rice, rather than wheat, reigns supreme. Sometimes rice will be the only starch served at a meal, but at other meals the breads made from rice will be served, such as the

thin, crisp Dosas (see page 243) or the steamed *idlis*.

If any generalization is possible, it is that rice is served with more liquid, soup-like dishes, such as Rasam (see page 71) and Sambhar (see page 82), and bread with the drier mixtures, such as Rogan Josh (see page 129).

For many Indians, especially southerners, and most foreigners, an Indian meal without rice is unimaginable. Mounds of rice, in numerous varieties and grades, are a feature of all Indian markets, and cooking it is second nature for home cooks. Long-grain Himalayan basmati rice is used for recipes in this book, but Patna rice, grown around the northern Indian town of the same name, is also suitable.

For an everyday rice recipe, try the Basmati Rice on page 26, but when there's time to make an effort, Spiced Basmati Rice (see page 232) has a fantastic fragrance and flavor that reflects Indian cooks' deft use of spices. Lemon Rice (see page 228) and Coconut Rice (see page 231) add the tastes of sunny southern India to any meal, while Fruit and Nut Pilaf (see page 227), with its spices, colorful dried fruits, and rich pistachios, evokes the lavish cooking of Moghul kitchens without the lengthy preparation of a biryani. A pilaf will transform a simple roast chicken into a maharajah's feast.

The real stars of Indian meals, however, are the chutneys, with their mixed textures and flavors. The word "chutney" is an Anglicization of the Hindi word *chatni*, meaning "freshly ground relish." Like Western relishes, chutneys can be raw or cooked,

finely chopped or chunky, and include many ingredients from fresh coconut, fruits, and herbs, to seeds, spices, dals, and so on. The possibilities are only limited by imagination. Mango chutney, familiar from all Indian restaurant and takeout meals, is a holdover from the British Raj. When colonial officers and their families returned home and meals seemed bland, a market developed for commercial brands that were shipped to Britain. Today, these are widely

Overleaf Rice-farming is dominated by manual labor and rice fields have to be tended to almost daily

Mango chutney is a holdover from the British Raj

available in supermarkets and Indian food stores, but the recipe on page 248 is a fresh, lighter version.

The other chutney recipes in this chapter reflect the diversity served in India. Coconut Sambal (see page 247) has a coarse texture, while Cilantro Chutney (see page 245), with ginger and chili, is a burst of fresh flavors. Chili and Onion Chutney (see page 246) and Raita (see page 244) are the perfect accompaniments for *tandoori* recipes.

fruit and nut pilaf

shahi mewa pullao

A feast for your eyes as well as your palate! Religious festivals of all beliefs dot the calendar throughout the year in India, and on most of these occasions special food adds to the festivities. This colorful Moghul dish can be part of a vegetarian feast, and is favored during the winter months in the north when fresh fruits aren't available. To mark an occasion, this would be served with Parathas (see page 239) rather than Chapatis (see page 236).

SERVES 4–6

scant 1¹/₄ cups basmati rice

2 cups water

¹/₂ tsp saffron threads

1 tsp salt

2 tbsp Ghee (see page 253) or vegetable or peanut oil

generous ¹/₃ cup blanched almonds

1 onion, thinly sliced

1 cinnamon stick, broken in half

seeds from 4 green cardamom pods

1 tsp cumin seeds

1 tsp black peppercorns, lightly crushed

2 bay leaves

3 tbsp finely chopped dried mango

3 tbsp finely chopped dried apricots

2 tbsp golden raisins

generous ¹/₃ cup pistachios, chopped

1 Rinse the basmati rice in several changes of water until the water runs clear, then let soak for 30 minutes. Drain and set aside until ready to cook.

2 Boil the water in a small pan. Add the saffron threads and salt, remove from the heat, and set aside to infuse

3 Melt the ghee in a flameproof casserole or large pan with a tight-fitting lid over medium-high heat. Add the almonds and stir them around until golden brown, then immediately use a slotted spoon to scoop them out of the casserole.

4 Add the onion to the casserole and sauté, stirring frequently, for 5–8 minutes until golden, but not brown. Add the spices and bay leaves to the pan and stir them around for about 30 seconds.

5 Add the rice to the casserole and stir until the grains are coated with ghee. Add the saffron-infused water and bring to a boil. Reduce the heat to as low as possible, stir in the dried fruits, and cover the casserole tightly. Simmer, without lifting the lid, for 8–10 minutes until the grains are tender and all the liquid is absorbed.

6 Turn off the heat and use 2 forks to mix the almonds and pistachios into the rice. Adjust the seasoning, if necessary. Re-cover the pan and let stand for 5 minutes*.

*cook's tip

If this dish, or any of the following rice recipes, are ready before you want to serve, place a clean dish towel between the rice and lid and let the rice stand for up to 20 minutes after you stir in the nuts in Step 6. The dish towel will absorb the steam and prevent the rice from becoming soggy.

228

lemon rice
nimbu bhaat

This colorful dish, popular in southern India, is ideal to serve with most fish dishes, as well as spiced meat dishes such as Lamb with Cauliflower (see page 141) and Lamb Shanks Marathani (see page 142).

SERVES 4–6

scant 1¼ cups basmati rice

2 tbsp Ghee (see page 253) or vegetable or peanut oil

1 tsp nigella seeds

2 cups water

juice and finely grated rind of 1 large lemon

1½ tsp salt

¼ tsp ground turmeric

1 Rinse the basmati rice in several changes of water until the water runs clear, then let soak for 30 minutes. Drain and set aside until ready to cook.

2 Melt the ghee in a flameproof casserole or large pan with a tight-fitting lid over medium-high heat. Add the nigella seeds to the rice and stir until all the grains are coated in ghee. Add the water and bring to a boil.

3 Reduce the heat to as low as possible, stir in half the lemon juice, salt, and turmeric, and cover the casserole tightly. Simmer, without lifting the lid, for 8–10 minutes until the grains are tender and all the liquid is absorbed.

4 Turn off the heat and use 2 forks to mix the lemon rind and remaining juice into the rice. Adjust the seasoning, if necessary. Re-cover the casserole and let the rice stand for 5 minutes*.

*cook's tip
To make a lemon and cashew rice, melt the ghee as in Step 2, add a generous ⅓ cup cashew nuts, and stir them around for 30 seconds, or until golden brown. Immediately use a slotted spoon to remove them from the casserole so they do not become too brown. Add 1 teaspoon fenugreek seeds with the nigella seeds and continue with the recipe. Stir the cashew nuts into the rice in Step 4 with the lemon rind and juice, then re-cover the pan and let stand for 5 minutes. Serve garnished with chopped fresh mint.

Car ownership has been rising very quickly in India, and cars are now common even outside the main cities

Regarded as the "fruit of the gods," coconut not only plays a major role in southern Indian kitchens, but also in Hindu religious ceremonies, where it can be used to symbolize a full, rich life. Fittingly, this dish is ideal for all special occasions.

coconut rice
thengai sadaam

231

*cook's tip

The mustard oil is heated and then cooled in Step 3 to reduce the pungency of its flavor. If you prefer to use vegetable or peanut oil, you can skip this step.

SERVES 4–6

scant 1¹⁄₄ cups basmati rice

2 cups water

2¹⁄₄ oz/60 g creamed coconut

2 tbsp mustard oil*

1¹⁄₂ tsp salt

1 Rinse the basmati rice in several changes of water until the water runs clear, then let soak for 30 minutes. Drain and set aside until ready to cook.

2 Bring the water to a boil in a small pan, stir in the creamed coconut until it dissolves, and then set aside.

3 Heat the mustard oil in a large skillet or pan with a lid over high heat until it smokes. Turn off the heat and let the mustard oil cool completely.

4 When you are ready to cook, reheat the mustard oil over medium-high heat. Add the rice and stir until all the grains are coated in oil. Add the water with the dissolved coconut and bring to a boil.

5 Reduce the heat to as low as possible, stir in the salt, and cover the pan tightly. Simmer, without lifting the lid, for 8–10 minutes until the grains are tender and all the liquid is absorbed.

6 Turn off the heat and use 2 forks to mix the rice. Adjust the seasoning, if necessary. Re-cover the pan and let the rice stand for 5 minutes.

Integral to Indian cooking, spices are often bought in bulk at the local market.

232 spiced basmati rice
chunke hue chawal

This delicately flavored dish comes from Rajasthan and has never fallen from favor since the days of Moghul rule. It is excellent to serve with lamb dishes.

SERVES 4–6

scant 1¼ cups basmati rice

2 tbsp Ghee (see page 253) or vegetable or peanut oil

5 green cardamom pods, lightly cracked

5 cloves

2 bay leaves

½ cinnamon stick

1 tsp fennel seeds

½ tsp black mustard seeds

2 cups water

1½ tsp salt

2 tbsp chopped fresh cilantro

pepper

1 Rinse the basmati rice in several changes of water until the water runs clear, then let soak for 30 minutes. Drain and set aside until ready to cook.

2 Melt the ghee in a flameproof casserole or large pan with a tight-fitting lid over medium-high heat. Add the spices and stir for 30 seconds. Stir the rice into the casserole so the grains are coated with ghee. Stir in the water and salt and bring to a boil.

3 Reduce the heat to as low as possible and cover the casserole tightly. Simmer, without lifting the lid, for 8–10 minutes until the grains are tender and all the liquid is absorbed.

4 Turn off the heat and use 2 forks to mix in the cilantro. Adjust the seasoning, if necessary. Re-cover the pan and let stand for 5 minutes*.

*cook's tip

For spiced saffron basmati rice, lightly toast 1 teaspoon saffron threads in a dry skillet over medium-high heat until you can smell the aroma, then immediately tip them out of the pan. Bring the water to a boil while the rice soaks, stir in the saffron threads and the salt, and set aside to infuse. Add the golden saffron-flavored water to the recipe in Step 2, as above, and follow the remaining recipe.

The Indians use their extensive inland waterways to transport food and materials

naans

naans

These leavened breads have been baked in India since the days of Moghul rule, traditionally by slapping the rolled and shaped dough against the hot inside of a charcoal-heated tandoor oven. As it is unlikely you have a tandoor oven at home, you won't be able produce identical breads to those at your favorite Indian restaurant, but these are very close. Just be sure to preheat your oven with a cookie sheet inside to its highest setting in plenty of time.

MAKES 10

6¹⁄₂ cups strong white flour

1 tbsp baking powder

1 tsp sugar

1 tsp salt

1¹⁄₄ cups water, heated to 122°F/50°C

1 egg, beaten

4 tbsp Ghee (see page 253), melted, plus a little extra
   for rolling out and brushing

1 Sift the flour, baking powder, sugar, and salt into a large mixing bowl and make a well in the center. Mix together the water and egg, beating until the egg breaks up and is blended with the liquid.

2 Slowly add the liquid mixture to the well in the dry ingredients, using your fingers to draw in the flour from the side, until a stiff, heavy dough forms. Shape the dough into a ball and return it to the bowl.

3 Soak a clean dish towel in hot water, then wring it out and use it to cover the bowl, tucking the ends of the dish towel under the bowl. Set the bowl aside to let the dough rest for 30 minutes.

4 Turn out the dough on to a counter brushed with melted ghee and flatten the dough. Gradually sprinkle the dough with the melted ghee and knead to work it in, little by little, until it is completely incorporated. Shape the dough into 10 equal balls.

5 Resoak the dish towel in hot water and wring it out again, then place it over the dough balls and let rest and rise for 1 hour.

6 Meanwhile, put 1 or 2 cookie sheets in the oven and preheat the oven to 450°F/230°C or its highest setting.

7 Use a lightly greased rolling pin to roll the dough balls into teardrop shapes, about ¹⁄₈ inch/3 mm thick. Use crumpled paper towels to lightly rub the hot cookie sheets with ghee. Arrange the naans on the cookie sheets and bake for 5–6 minutes until they are golden brown and lightly puffed. As you take the naans out of the oven, brush with melted ghee and serve at once*.

*cook's tip

For garlic and nigella seed naans, scatter the dough just before it is baked with 3 very thinly sliced garlic cloves and 2 tablespoons nigella seeds. For sesame naans, sprinkle the dough just before it is baked with 2 tablespoons sesame seeds. For cilantro naans, knead 2 oz/55 g finely chopped fresh cilantro into the dough after the ghee is incorporated in Step 4.

236

chapatis
chapatis

Chapatis are the everyday bread for millions of Indians, eaten by virtually everyone from the richest to the very poor. The soft, malleable texture makes these flatbreads ideal for mopping up "gravies," as Indian sauces are known, and for scooping up bite-size portions of food, doing away with knives and forks. Unleavened chapatis are traditionally made with atta, a type of Indian whole-wheat flour that is sold in Asian food stores, but ordinary whole-wheat flour is fine if you sift out the gritty pieces of bran first. Indian cooks, who are very accomplished at preparing these one after another as a meal is being served, use a short, tapered rolling pin that is thicker in the center to shape the dough, then cook it on a hot, flat griddle called a tava. An ordinary rolling pin and skillet, however, work just as well.

MAKES 6

1¹/₂ **cups whole-wheat flour, sifted,**
  plus extra for dusting
¹/₂ **tsp salt**
²/₃–³/₄ **cup water**
melted Ghee (see page 253), for brushing

1 Mix the flour and salt together in a large bowl and make a well in the center. Gradually stir in enough water to make a stiff dough.

2 Turn out the dough on to a lightly floured counter and knead for 10 minutes, or until it is smooth and elastic. Shape the dough into a ball and place it in the cleaned bowl, then cover with a damp dish towel and let rest for 20 minutes.

3 Divide the dough into 6 equal pieces. Lightly flour your hands and roll each piece of dough into a ball. Meanwhile, heat a large, ungreased tava, skillet, or griddle over high heat until very hot and a splash of water "dances" when it hits the surface.

4 Working with 1 ball of dough at a time, flatten the dough between your palms, then roll it out on a lightly floured counter into a 7-inch/18-cm circle. Slap the dough on to the hot pan and cook until brown flecks appear on the bottom. Flip the dough over and repeat on the other side*.

5 Flip the dough over again and use a bunched up dish towel to press down all around the edge. This pushes the steam in the chapati around, causing the chapati to puff up. Continue cooking until the bottom is golden brown, then flip over and repeat this step on the other side.

6 Brush the chapati with melted ghee and serve, then repeat with the remaining dough balls. Chapatis are best served at once, as soon as they come out of the pan, but they can be kept warm wrapped in foil for about 20 minutes.

*cook's tip

Do not be tempted to flip the chapatis more times than specified above, or they will not puff up and will become heavy. Indian cooks use their fingers to flip the dough over in Steps 4 and 5, but unless you have asbestos fingers, use a pair of tongs or a metal spatula.

parathas
parathas

These are pan-fried, unleavened breads for special occasions and religious festivals. Made with lots of melted ghee, parathas have a flaky texture and are too rich for everyday meals—unless, of course, you don't worry about your waistline! For an Indian-style breakfast, try parathas with a bowl of thick yogurt.

MAKES 8

1¹/₂ **cups whole-wheat flour, sifted,**
   plus extra for dusting
¹/₂ **tsp salt**
²/₃–³/₄ **cup water**
5 oz/140 g Ghee (see page 253), melted

1 Mix the flour and salt together in a large bowl and make a well in the center. Gradually stir in enough water to make a stiff dough.

2 Turn out the dough on to a lightly floured counter and knead for 10 minutes, or until it is smooth and elastic. Shape the dough into a ball and place it in the cleaned bowl, then cover with a damp dish towel and let rest for 20 minutes.

3 Divide the dough into 8 equal pieces. Lightly flour your hands and roll each piece of dough into a ball.

4 Working with one ball of dough at a time, roll it out on a lightly floured counter until it is a 5-inch/ 13-cm circle. Brush the top of the dough with about 1¹/₂ teaspoons of the melted ghee. Fold the circle in half to make a half-moon shape and brush the top again with melted ghee. Fold the half-moon shape in half again to make a triangle. Press the layers together.

5 Roll out the triangle on a lightly floured counter into a larger triangle that is about 7 inches/18 cm on each side. Flip the dough back and forth between your hands a couple of times, then cover with a damp dish towel. Continue until all the dough is shaped and rolled.

6 Meanwhile, heat a large, ungreased tava, skillet, or griddle over high heat until very hot and a splash of water "dances" when it hits the surface. Place a paratha in the pan and cook until bubbles appear on the surface.

7 Use tongs to flip the paratha over and brush the surface with melted ghee. Continue cooking until the bottom is golden brown, then flip the paratha over again and smear with more melted ghee. Use a wooden spoon or spatula to press down on the surface of the paratha so it cooks evenly.

8 Brush with more melted ghee and serve, then repeat with the remaining parathas. Parathas are best served at once, as soon as they come out of the pan, but they can be kept warm wrapped in foil for about 20 minutes.

Headgear is more than just a defense against heat and cold, it can be a symbol of religion, origin, or social status

240 pooris
puris

These deep-fried breads puff up to look like balloons when they go into the hot oil, and are perfect for serving with most "veg" and "non-veg" curries. Children love watching these cooking. Pooris will be made in huge quantities to serve at Hindu weddings and special occasions. They also make a traditional, if somewhat unexpected, accompaniment to Shrikhand with Pomegranate (see page 207).

MAKES 12

1¹/₂ cups whole-wheat flour, sifted,
  plus extra for dusting

¹/₂ teaspoon salt

2 tbsp ghee, melted

¹/₃–²/₃ cup water

vegetable or peanut oil, for deep-frying

1 Put the flour and salt into a bowl and drizzle the ghee over the surface. Gradually stir in the water until a stiff dough forms.

2 Turn out the dough on to a lightly floured counter and knead for 10 minutes, or until it is smooth and elastic. Shape the dough into a ball and place it in the cleaned bowl, then cover with a damp dish towel and let rest for 20 minutes.

3 Divide the dough into 12 equal pieces and roll each into a ball. Working with one ball of dough at a time, flatten the dough between your palms, then thinly roll it out on a lightly floured counter into a 5-inch/13-cm circle. Continue until all the dough balls are rolled out.

4 Heat at least 3 inches/7.5 cm oil in a kadhai, wok, deep-fat fryer, or large skillet until it reaches 350°F/180°C, or until a cube of bread browns in 30 seconds. Drop one poori into the hot fat and deep-fry for about 10 seconds, or until it puffs up. Use 2 large spoons to flip the poori over and spoon some hot oil over the top.

5 Use the 2 spoons to lift the poori from the oil and let any excess oil drip back into the pan. Drain the poori on crumpled paper towels and serve at once. Continue until all the pooris are cooked, making sure the oil returns to the correct temperature before you add another poori.

cook's tip
To make mini pooris to use in Bhel Poori (see page 44), roll out the dough as in Step 3, then use a lightly greased 1¹/₂-inch/4-cm cookie cutter to stamp out smaller circles.

In India, the streets are packed with vendors selling goods or their services

*In southern India, these ultra-thin, crisp crêpes are
served with Cilantro Chutney or Coconut Sambal
(see pages 245 and 247) for snacks, or rolled around
a spicy potato mixture to make the popular Dosa
Masala (see page 84), which is even served for
breakfast. As dosas are cooked in a thin layer of
ghee, they have a rich flavor. An experienced dosa
maker will flip these on the hot tava, an Indian
griddle, one after another without any apparent
effort. For a novice dosa maker, however, it is a
slower process. Try a practice batch first, and don't
be tempted to flip a dosa before it has cooked long
enough to become crisp on the bottom. It also helps
to use the largest, flattest pan you have. A skillet
can be used, but a griddle or crêpe pan makes the
job easier. In India, it's not uncommon to be served
dosas that are up to 16 inches/40 cm across, but
this recipe makes them in a more manageable size.
Remember to start the batter a day in advance
because it soaks overnight.*

dosas 243
dosas

MAKES ABOUT 8 DOSAS
salt
scant ²/₃ cup basmati rice, rinsed
¹/₃ cup split black lentils (urad dal chilke)
¹/₄ tsp fenugreek seeds
¹/₂ cup water
2 tbsp Ghee (see page 253), melted

1 Bring a pan of salted water to a boil, add the
basmati rice, and boil for 5 minutes, then drain.
Put the rice, split black lentils, and fenugreek seeds in
a bowl with water to cover and let soak overnight.

2 The next day, strain the rice and lentils, reserving
the soaking liquid. Put the rice and lentils in a food
processor with 5 tbsp of the water and whiz until
a smooth, sludgy gray paste forms. Slowly add the
remaining water.

3 Cover the bowl with a dish towel that has been
soaked in hot water and wrung out and leave
to ferment in a warm place for 5–6 hours until small
bubbles appear all over the surface.

4 Stir the mixture and add as much extra water as
necessary to get a consistency of light cream. Add
salt to taste. The amount of salt you need depends on
how "sour"-tasting the batter is.

5 Heat the flattest, largest pan you have over a
high heat until a splash of water "dances" when
it hits the surface, then brush the surface with melted
ghee. Put a ladleful of batter in the center of the pan
and use the bottom of the ladle to spread it out as
thinly as possible in concentric circles, then let cook
for 2 minutes until it is golden brown and crisp
on the bottom.

6 Flip the dosa over* and continue cooking for an
additional 2 minutes. Turn out of the pan and keep
warm if you are going to wrap around a filling, or let
cool. Continue until all the batter has been used.

*cook's tip
Although dosas look a little like French crêpes, they cook
differently and do not slide around in the pan. To flip
the dosa in Step 6, you need to slide a thin metal tool
underneath to loosen it from the pan. A metal spatula
can be used, but a clean paint scraper actually works
more efficiently.

244 raita
raita

This is the all-purpose, everyday accompaniment that is served with almost any spicy dish and the variations are endless (see below). The creaminess of the yogurt and the coolness of the cucumber help to temper the heat of spicy dishes.

SERVES 4–6

1 large piece cucumber, about 10$\frac{1}{2}$ oz/300 g, rinsed

1 teaspoon salt

1$\frac{3}{4}$ cups plain yogurt

$\frac{1}{2}$ teaspoon sugar

pinch of ground cumin

2 tablespoons chopped fresh cilantro or mint

chili powder, to garnish

1 Lay a clean dish towel flat on the counter. Coarsely grate the unpeeled cucumber directly on to the dish towel. Sprinkle with $\frac{1}{2}$ teaspoon of the salt, then gather up the dish towel and squeeze until all the excess moisture is removed from the cucumber.

2 Put the yogurt into a bowl and beat in the remaining $\frac{1}{2}$ teaspoon of salt, along with the sugar and cumin. Stir in the grated cucumber. Taste and add extra seasoning, if you like. Cover and chill until ready to serve.

3 Stir in the chopped cilantro and transfer to a serving bowl. Sprinkle with chili powder and serve*.

* cook's tip

For a variation, stir in 2 seeded and finely chopped tomatoes or 4 finely chopped scallions with the cilantro or mint. Ground coriander or ginger can also be added to taste. To make a banana raita, peel and slice 3 bananas directly into the yogurt, then stir in 2 seeded and chopped fresh green chilies and 1 tablespoon garam masala. Add a little lemon rind and juice, if you like. Cover and chill until required, then stir in the chopped fresh cilantro or mint just before serving.

cilantro chutney
hare dhaniye ki chutney

This is an example of one of the uncooked, fresh-tasting chutneys that are served with every meal or snack throughout the day in Kerala, starting with breakfast. The bright green cilantro, fresh coconut, and chili capture the flavors of the region.

MAKES ABOUT 1 1/3 CUPS

1 1/2 tbsp lemon juice

1 1/2 tbsp water

3 oz/85 g fresh cilantro leaves and stems, coarsely chopped

2 tbsp chopped fresh coconut

1 small shallot, very finely chopped

1/4-inch/5-mm piece fresh gingerroot, chopped

1 fresh green chili, seeded and chopped

1/2 tsp sugar

1/2 tsp salt

pinch of pepper

1 Put the lemon juice and water in a small food processor, add half the cilantro, and whiz until it is blended and a slushy paste forms. Gradually add the remaining cilantro and whiz until it is all blended, scraping down the sides of the processor, if necessary. If you don't have a processor that will cope with this small amount, use a pestle and mortar, adding the cilantro in small amounts.

2 Add the remaining ingredients and continue whizzing until they are all finely chopped and blended. Taste and adjust any of the seasonings, if you like. Transfer to a nonmetallic bowl, cover, and chill for up to 3 days before serving*.

*cook's tip

For a cooling cilantro raita, stir 1 1/4 cups plain yogurt into the chutney and chill for at least 1 hour before serving. Sprinkle with plenty of chopped fresh cilantro just before serving.

246

chili and onion chutney
mirch aur pyaaz ki chutney

For those who really like spicy hot food, this fresh chutney packs quite a punch. It's hot, zingy, and can bring tears to your eyes if you don't seed the chilies. Try this as an accompaniment to Tandoori Chicken (see page 156) or Chicken Tikka Masala (see page 161). Gujaratis will include the chili seeds and serve this at all meals, eating it in the summer like a snack with poppadoms or Pooris (see page 240).

MAKES ABOUT 1 1/3 CUPS

1–2 fresh green chilies, seeded or not, to taste, and finely chopped

1 small Thai chili, seeded or not, to taste, and finely chopped

1 tbsp white wine or cider vinegar

2 onions, finely chopped

2 tbsp fresh lemon juice

1 tbsp sugar

3 tbsp chopped fresh cilantro, mint, or parsley, or a combination of herbs

salt

chili flower, to garnish

1 Put the chilies in a small nonmetallic bowl with the vinegar, stir around, and then drain. Return the chilies to the bowl and stir in the onions, lemon juice, sugar, and herbs, then add salt to taste.

2 Let stand at room temperature or cover and chill for 15 minutes. Garnish with the chili flower before serving the chutney*.

*cook's tip

For a chili and onion raita, stir 1 1/4 cups plain yogurt into the chutney mixture and chill for at least 1 hour. Stir before serving and sprinkle with fresh herbs.

coconut sambal
nariyal sambal

Coconuts grow in abundance along the gently flowing backwaters in Kerala and slightly crunchy, fresh chutneys like this are served at many meals. Serve this with poppadoms as a snack or use it to accompany simply broiled fresh seafood. In Kerala and Tamil Nadu it is served with the crisp, thin Dosas (see page 243).

MAKES ABOUT 1 CUP

1/2 **fresh coconut, about 4 oz/115 g of meat,**
  or 1 1/4 cups dry unsweetened coconut

2 **fresh green chilies, seeded or not,**
  to taste, and chopped

1-**inch/2.5-cm piece fresh gingeroot, peeled**
  and finely chopped

4 **tbsp chopped fresh cilantro**

2 **tbsp lemon juice, or to taste**

2 **shallots, very finely chopped**

1 If you are using a whole coconut, use a hammer and nail to punch a hole in the "eye" of the coconut, then pour out the water from the inside and reserve. Use the hammer to break the coconut in half, then peel half and chop.

2 Put the coconut and chilies in a small food processor and whiz for about 30 seconds until finely chopped. Add the ginger, cilantro, and lemon juice and whiz again.

3 If the mixture seems too dry, whiz in about 1 tablespoon coconut water or water. Stir in the shallots and serve at once, or cover and chill until required. This will keep its fresh flavor, covered, in the refrigerator for up to 3 days".

*cook's tip

For a punchier-tasting chutney, stir in 1/2 tablespoon black mustard seeds with the shallots. A little ground cumin is also a good addition.

248

mango chutney
aam ki chutney

This light, spiced chutney is about as far as one can get from the thick, overly sweet mango chutney in jars. It adds the sunny flavor of Goa and southern India to any Indian meal.

MAKES ABOUT 1½ CUPS

1 large mango, about 14 oz/400 g, peeled, pitted, and finely chopped

2 tbsp lime juice

1 tbsp vegetable or peanut oil

2 shallots, finely chopped

1 garlic clove, finely chopped

2 fresh green chilies, seeded and finely sliced

1 tsp black mustard seeds

1 tsp coriander seeds

5 tbsp grated jaggery or brown sugar

5 tbsp white wine vinegar

1 tsp salt

pinch of ground ginger

1 Put the mango in a nonmetallic bowl with the lime juice and set aside.

2 Heat the oil in a large skillet or pan over medium-high heat. Add the shallots and sauté for 3 minutes. Add the garlic and chilies and stir for an additional 2 minutes, or until the shallots are soft, but not brown. Add the mustard and coriander seeds, then stir around.

3 Add the mango to the pan with the jaggery, vinegar, salt, and ginger and stir around. Reduce the heat to its lowest setting and simmer for 10 minutes until the liquid thickens and the mango becomes sticky.

4 Remove from the heat and let cool completely. Transfer to an airtight container, cover, and chill for 3 days before using. Store in the refrigerator and use within 1 week.

tamarind chutney

imli ki chutney

There isn't any mistaking the fresh, sour taste of tamarind: it adds a distinctive flavor to many dishes, especially those from southern India. More like a sauce than a thick chutney, this sweet-and-sour tasting mixture is essential to serve with Bhel Poori (see page 44) and Vegetarian Samosas (see page 40). It also goes particularly well with pan-fried fish.

MAKES ABOUT 1 1/2 CUPS

3 1/2 oz/100 g tamarind pulp, chopped

2 cups water

1/2 **Thai chili, or to taste, seeded and chopped**

generous 1/4 **cup brown sugar, or to taste**

1/2 **tsp salt**

1 Put the tamarind and water in a heavy-bottom pan over high heat and bring to a boil. Reduce the heat to the lowest setting and simmer for 25 minutes, stirring occasionally to break up the tamarind pulp, or until tender.

2 Tip the tamarind pulp into a strainer and use a wooden spoon to push the pulp into the rinsed-out pan.

3 Stir in the chili, sugar, and salt and continue simmering for an additional 10 minutes or until the desired consistency is reached. Let cool slightly, then stir in extra sugar or salt, to taste.

4 Let cool completely, then cover tightly and chill for up to 3 days, or freeze.

An Indian man stands against a dramatic background of hills in Kumbulgarh

250

chili bon-bon
badi mirchi ka meetha achaa

Simple to make, this condiment adds an intriguing flavor to any simply broiled or roasted meat or seafood. "Invented" by British army cooks during the Raj, you can still find this today on many Anglo-Indian tables.

MAKES 1¼ CUPS
1¼ cups medium or dry sherry
1 or 2 Thai chilies, to taste

1 Pour the sherry into a sterilized jar. Make several long slits in the chilies, then add them to the sherry. Seal the jar, shake well, and set aside for at least 3 days before using. Store in the refrigerator and use within a month.

Men in India have traditionally grown moustaches as a sign of masculinity

garam masala
garam masala

"Garam" means "hot" and "masala" means "mixed spices," so this is an aromatic mixture of hot spices, but not "hot" as in the fiery, spicy hot meaning of the word, but rather as in warming to heat the body. Unlike most other spices and masala mixtures, garam masala is usually added toward the end of cooking for a savory, fragrant taste. You can buy garam masala in supermarkets and Asian food stores, but if you do lots of Indian cooking it is fun to make your own mixture. Use this recipe as a starting point, but experiment with the quantities until you get a mixture that you like. Garam masala is almost always added in small amounts, so to prevent the flavor from dulling, do not make a large quantity. Indian cooks often make a fresh batch for each meal.

*cook's tip

If you don't have a small grinder that you use exclusively for spices, whiz a few pieces of torn white bread in the grinder after you use it for spices. The bread will absorb much of the residual aromas.

MAKES ABOUT 6 TABLESPOONS

2 bay leaves, crumbled

2 cinnamon sticks, broken in half

seeds from 8 green cardamom pods

2 tbsp cumin seeds

1½ tbsp coriander seeds

1½ tsp black peppercorns

1 tsp cloves

¼ tsp ground cloves

1 Heat a dry skillet over high heat until a splash of water "dances" when it hits the surface. Reduce the heat to medium, add the bay leaves, cinnamon sticks, cardamom pods, cumin seeds, coriander seeds, peppercorns, and cloves and dry roast, stirring constantly, until the cumin seeds look dark golden brown and you can smell the aromas.

2 Immediately tip the spices out of the pan and let cool. Use a spice grinder* or pestle and mortar to grind the spices to a fine powder. Stir in the ground cloves. Store in an airtight container for up to 2 months.

252

paneer
paneer

For India's millions of vegetarians, this firm white cheese is a main source of daily protein. Although paneer has a bland flavor on its own, it is similar to Asian tofu in that it absorbs flavors when cooked with other ingredients. In all of India, except in the south, paneer is used in both savory and sweet dishes. It is often partnered with lentils or dried beans or peas and vegetables, and its firm texture means it is also ideal for broiling and roasting. Fresh paneer is sold in Asian food stores, but it is straightforward to make at home.

MAKES ABOUT 12 OZ/350 G

2 quarts milk

6 tbsp lemon juice

1 Pour the milk into a large, heavy-bottom pan over high heat and bring to a full boil. Remove the pan from the heat and stir in the lemon juice. Return the pan to the heat and continue boiling for an additional minute until the curds and whey separate and the liquid is clear.

2 Remove the pan from the heat and set aside for an hour or so, until the milk is completely cool. Meanwhile, line a strainer set over a bowl with a piece of cheesecloth large enough to hang over the edge.

3 Pour the cold curds and whey* into the cheesecloth, then gather up the edges and squeeze out all the excess moisture.

4 Use a piece of string to tie the cheesecloth tightly around the curds in a ball. Put the ball in a bowl and place a plate on top. Place a can of beans or tomatoes on the plate to weigh down the curds, then let stand for at least 12 hours in the refrigerator. The curds will press into a compact mass that can be cut. The paneer will keep for up to 3 days in the refrigerator.

*cook's tip

The whey by-product of paneer-making can be discarded, but clever Indian cooks add it to the cooking water for vegetables or lentils.

ghee
ghee

The traditional rich flavor of many Indian dishes, especially those from the northern regions, comes, at least in part, from cooking with ghee, an Indian form of clarified butter. To make ghee, the golden butter fat and milk solids are separated over heat, and then simmered a little longer until the milk solids turn light brown, which develops a slightly nutty flavor. It is this nutty flavor that distinguishes ghee from clarified butter in the West. Ghee is the cooking fat of choice for many Indian cooks because of its flavor and because it doesn't burn at high temperatures. But, alas, its high cholesterol content means it is slowly being replaced on an everyday basis by a vegetable oil, such as sunflower or peanut. This is why many recipes in this book list oil as an alternative to ghee. Asian food stores sell tubs of ghee, but when you don't cook Indian every day and want an authentic flavor, it is easy to make.*

MAKES ABOUT 7 OZ/200 G

9 oz/250 g butter

1 Melt the butter in a large, heavy-bottom pan over medium heat and continue simmering until a thick foam appears on the surface.

2 Continue simmering, uncovered, for about 15–20 minutes*, or until the foam separates and the milk solids settle on the bottom and the liquid becomes clear and golden.

3 Meanwhile, line a strainer with a piece of cheesecloth and place the strainer over a bowl. Slowly pour the liquid through the cheesecloth, without disturbing the milk solids at the bottom of the pan. Discard the milk solids.

4 Let the ghee cool, then transfer it to a smaller container, cover, and chill. It will keep in the refrigerator for up to 4 weeks, or it can be frozen.

*cook's tip
Watch the simmering ghee closely in Step 2 because the milk solids on the bottom of the pan can burn quickly.

index

ESTE
CUERPO
ES
HUMANO

ANATOMÍA ESCRITA Y DIBUJADA
POR GRASSA TORO
Y JOSÉ LUIS CANO

thule

Con nuestro agradecimiento a Stella Ibáñez,
Marisa Jimeno, Alfredo Martínez,
Nubia Villamil, Christopher Yates y Joana Tortella.

Este cuerpo es humano

© 2009 Grassa Toro (texto)
© 2009 José Luis Cano (ilustraciones)
© 2009 Thule Ediciones, S.L.
      Alcalá de Guadaira, 26, bajos
      08020 Barcelona

Un proyecto de Arianna Squilloni
Director de colección: José Díaz
Diseño y maquetación: Jennifer Carná

ISBN: 978-84-92595-01-3

Impreso en China

www.thuleediciones.com

PRÓLOGO

Tenemos un cuerpo, pero no lo tenemos como tenemos un perro, una bicicleta o una falda; el perro nos acompaña, en la bicicleta nos subimos, la falda nos la ponemos y todo eso sucede porque están fuera. El cuerpo no está ni fuera ni dentro de nosotros, tenemos un cuerpo que es nuestro cuerpo que somos nosotros. Somos un cuerpo, cada uno el suyo.

Sabemos que somos un cuerpo porque el ser humano es capaz de saber cosas sobre sí mismo además de tener algún conocimiento acerca del resto de realidad. Como no podemos separarnos de nuestro cuerpo, salirnos y dejarlo ahí plantado (aunque, a veces, bien que nos gustaría), la posibilidad de conocerlo es contemplar el cuerpo de otro o una representación.

Contemplar otro cuerpo tiene alguna dificultad, no hay mucha gente dispuesta a quedarse quieta durante horas o durante días mientras alguien le está estudiando del pelo a la punta del pie. Además, por mucho que miremos, no veremos más allá de las formas exteriores y la superficie cutánea; la mayor parte de nuestro cuerpo permanece oculta.

Durante siglos, había que esperar el momento de la muerte para abrir en canal el cadáver, despedazarlo y, rápidamente, dibujar del natural huesos, músculos, órganos… Luego, ese dibujo podía reproducirse mediante grabados o formar parte de un libro impreso.

En 1896 cambió todo, se utilizaron por primera vez los rayos X para ver los huesos de la mano de un ser vivo sin necesidad de abrírsela. A partir de ese momento y gracias a la radiografía, el escáner y la resonancia magnética, podemos contemplar, cada día con más detalle, cómo somos por dentro sin agujerearnos para hacerlo. Las máquinas nos ofrecen abundante información, a nosotros nos queda interpretar qué significa; esta interpretación la hacemos con palabras, ponemos nombres a las partes, de la unión de imágenes del cuerpo y palabras que las nombran nacen los atlas de anatomía.

A los seres humanos nos resulta más fácil entender la realidad si la partimos en pedazos, ordenamos los pedazos, los clasificamos, los jerarquizamos. Los atlas de anatomía se construyen así, limitando, dividiendo: sistema muscular, aparato respiratorio, esqueleto… Esta manera de presentar el cuerpo no puede confundirnos, cada parte del cuerpo no está separada de las demás, ni actúa por su cuenta, ni desconoce qué está pasando en el resto; al contrario, todo nuestro cuerpo es una unidad, cada uno de nosotros es una unidad en la que cada elemento que podemos reconocer durante el estudio está relacionado con el resto de los elementos. Durante la realización de esta anatomía escrita e ilustrada hemos intentado no olvidarnos de esta integridad.

Este libro dice algo acerca de cómo estamos hechos y deja mucho sin decir; el resto puede descubrirse leyendo otros libros, viendo modelos tridimensionales físicos o virtuales o tocándonos, sin ir más lejos.

Este libro también dice algo de cómo somos y también deja mucho por decir. Decir cómo somos es más difícil que decir cómo estamos hechos, pero no podemos saber cómo somos si no sabemos cómo estamos hechos.

Este libro, por fin, dice algo de cómo nos vemos, nos reconocemos, nos pensamos. De esto dice poco, aunque dice más de lo que parece.

Lo mejor de este libro es que no dice todo. Así deja sitio para que otros digan.

LOS AUTORES

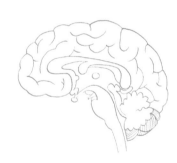

4

ÓRGANOS GENITALES

DONDE SE EMPIEZA POR EL PRINCIPIO

Pene, pene, pene, pene, pene, pene, pene y escroto, testículos, próstata y vesículas seminales. Órganos genitales masculinos.

Vagina, vagina, vagina, vagina, vagina, vagina, vagina y labios mayores, labios menores, clítoris, vestíbulo, glándulas vestibulares mayores, himen, monte de Venus, útero, trompas de Falopio y ovarios. Órganos genitales femeninos.

Los pies no se llaman pics porque sirvan para bailar; en cambio, los órganos genitales se llaman órganos genitales porque son capaces de proporcionar la materia necesaria para generar nueva vida.

Claro que puestos a buscar razones o etimologías también podrían llamarse órganos principales, pasionales, fundamentales, sensacionales, trascendentales, joviales y, en ese caso, tendríamos que corregir así:

Los testículos son los órganos ~~genitales~~ pasionales dedicados a la fabricación de espermatozoides. Las vesículas seminales y la próstata aportan líquido que sumado a los espermatozoides constituye el semen. La próstata es un órgano ~~genital~~ jovial. El pene es el órgano ~~genital~~ tras-

cendental externo del hombre, capaz de elevarse sobre un punto de apoyo localizado en la pelvis gracias a una acumulación de sangre en sus dos cuerpos cavernosos y capaz también de sacar el semen fuera del cuerpo.

La vulva es el órgano ~~genital~~ sensacional externo de la mujer. Está formado por labios mayores y labios menores, el clítoris, el vestíbulo, las glándulas vestibulares mayores, el himen y el monte de Venus. Los órganos ~~genitales~~ fundamentales internos son la vagina, el útero, las trompas y los ovarios. Los ovarios, órganos ~~genitales~~ principales, que están separados y no siempre en el mismo sitio (tampoco se van demasiado lejos), producen óvulos.

De la fecundación de un óvulo por un espermatozoide puede nacer un ser humano. Los seres humanos nacemos de otro ser humano, una mujer dentro de la cual pasamos nueve meses. Ese tiempo es el único de toda nuestra vida que pasamos dentro de alguien.

Los órganos genitales no saltan a la vista porque la mayoría de los seres humanos hemos decidido cubrirlos de lunes

a domingo, aunque no tengamos ningu-
na necesidad de hacerlo. Aún así, todo el
mundo sabe dónde están.

Además de principales, pasionales, fundamentales, sensacionales, trascendentales
o joviales, todos estos órganos son sexuales.

La sexualidad no es una parte del cuerpo,
ni una cosa, ni una idea, ni una época del
año, no es un lugar, ni un secreto, ni un
trabajo, ni un vestido, ni una obligación.
Lo más probable es que sea una circuns-
tancia y yo.

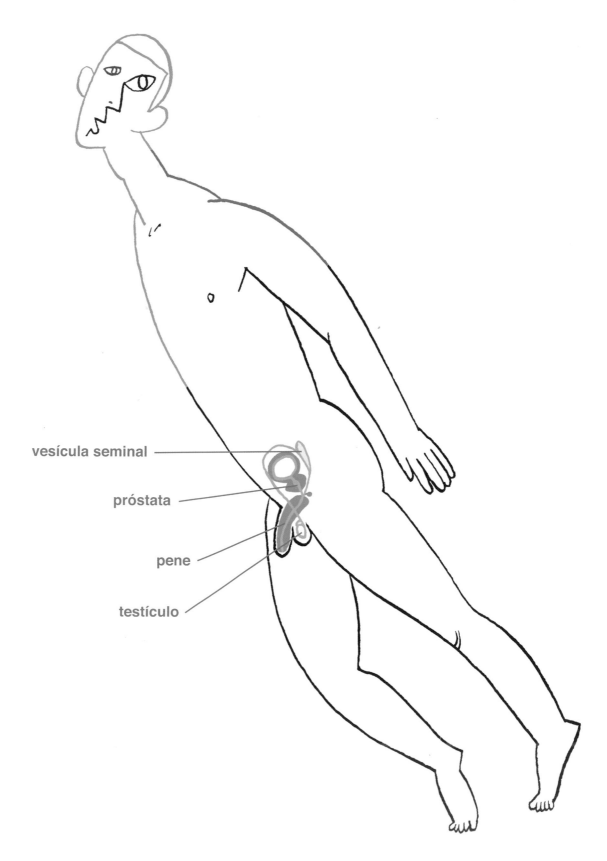

vesícula seminal

próstata

pene

testículo

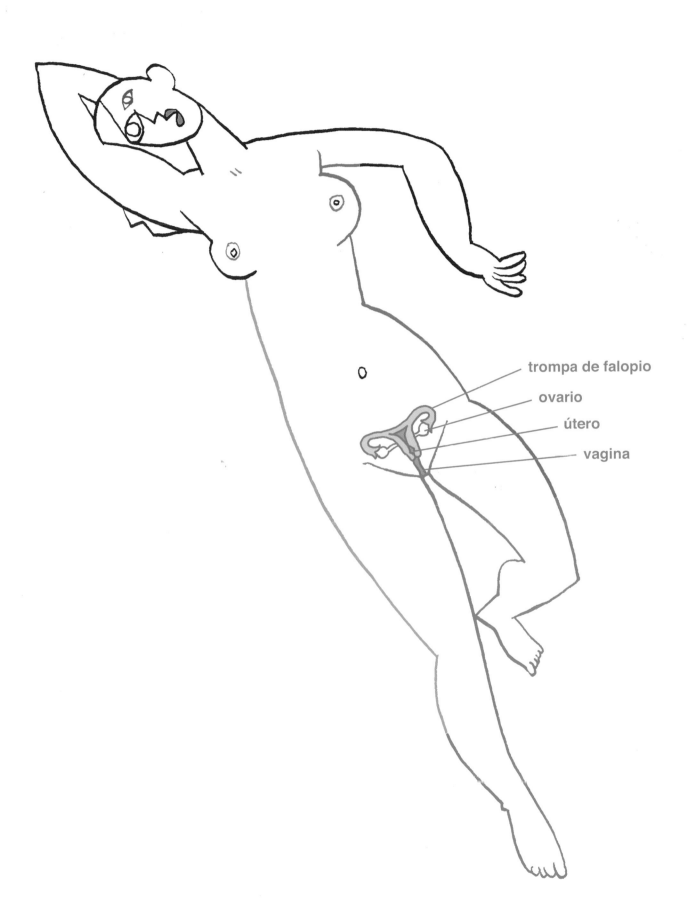

trompa de falopio

ovario

útero

vagina

Sistema nervioso

Donde se presentan algunas preguntas de difícil respuesta con la intención de no dar nada por sabido

¿Tienes hambre? ¿Por qué lo sabes?

¿Has pasado miedo al atardecer? ¿Por qué lo sabes?

¿Puedes volar? ¿Por qué lo sabes?

¿Cuándo sientes más cansancio, antes o después de llorar? ¿Por qué lo sabes?

¿Quieres a alguien que vive cerca de un sitio donde mana el agua? ¿Por qué lo sabes?

¿El rinoceronte es animal o idea? ¿Por qué lo sabes?

¿Dónde tienes el bulbo raquídeo, el cerebelo, el puente, el techo mesencefálico, el cerebro, el tálamo y el hipotálamo? ¿Por qué lo sabes?

¿Simpático y parasimpático son algo o son formas de ser algo? ¿Por qué lo sabes?

¿Es la misma amargura la de la despedida y la de la almendra? ¿Por qué lo sabes?

¿Qué quieres ganar? ¿Por qué lo sabes?

¿Te gustaría acariciar las dendritas de una neurona? ¿Por qué lo sabes?

¿Recuerdas cómo suena un grito al otro lado de la ventana? ¿Por qué lo sabes?

¿Estás de pie? ¿Por qué lo sabes? ¿Respirar es más importante que comer? ¿Por qué lo sabes?

¿Quieres acabar esta página o vas a dejarlo aquí? ¿Por qué lo sabes?

¿Es más importante por médula o por espinal? ¿Por qué lo sabes?

¿Cuánto ha pasado desde que soplaste la última vez? ¿Por qué lo sabes?

¿Puede el mundo estar fuera y dentro de ti? ¿Por qué lo sabes?

Todo lo que sabemos lo sabemos porque tenemos sistema nervioso, y tenemos sistema nervioso para procurarnos placer, y necesitamos el placer para estar vivos, que es lo único que tenemos que hacer cuando estamos vivos.

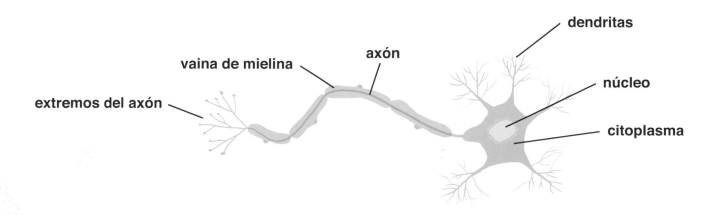

extremos del axón   vaina de mielina   axón   dendritas   núcleo   citoplasma

bulbo raquídeo

cerebelo

puente

techo mesencefálico

tálamo

hipotálamo

médula espinal

sistema nervioso vegetativo

nervio ciático

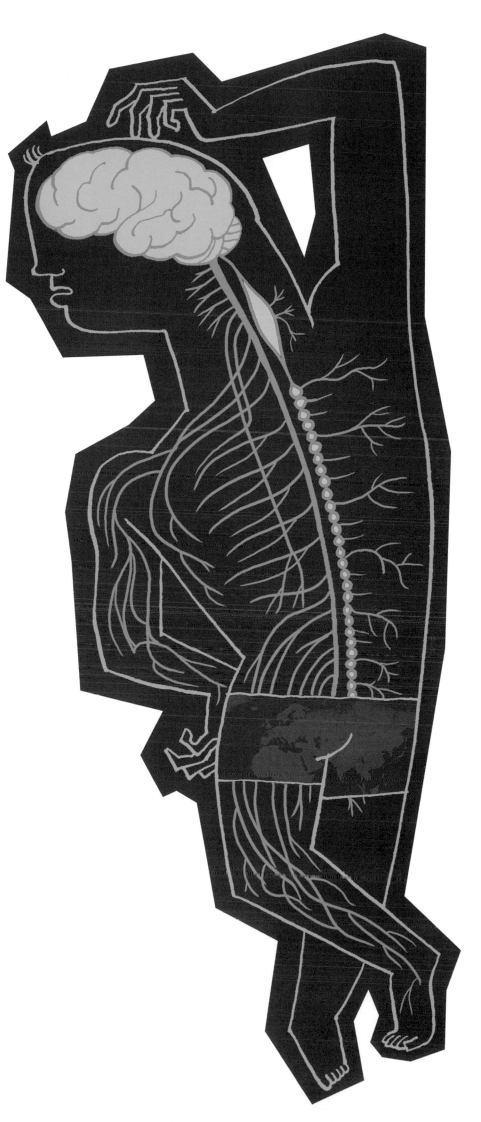

CEREBRO

DONDE SE RAZONA POR QUÉ NO TENEMOS QUE ASUSTARNOS DE NADA

No es nada extraño que los cerebros parezcan nueces; tampoco lo es que las nueces parezcan cerebros. Se parecen, no son iguales; una de las diferencias es que la nuez no sabe que se parece al cerebro y el cerebro sabe que se parece a la nuez. Otra diferencia es que cada día se comen en el mundo muchas más nueces que cerebros. La tercera diferencia tiene que ver con el tiempo de vida, una nuez vive poco menos de un año —un año humano, se entiende—, el cerebro vive hasta que se muere.

A veces, el cerebro se va muriendo por trozos y nos quedamos sin poder oler, o sin verlas venir, o sin distinguir el bien del mal; depende de qué trozo haya dejado de vivir. Cuando esto nos sucede, quien está a nuestro lado se preocupa. Claro que también podemos asustarnos cuando conocemos de qué es capaz un cerebro que esté vivo completamente. Porque un cerebro es capaz de cualquier cosa.

Y esto es como es porque nuestro cerebro es un enorme almacén de memoria que se acuerda de cómo éramos hace millones de años, cuando nos arrastrábamos; hace algo menos, cuando andábamos a cuatro patas; hace dos días, cuando nos pusimos a aplaudir. Y de esa memoria va sacando siempre que lo necesita, que es siempre. Así, no es de extrañar que, a veces, nos comportemos como víboras, otras como rinocerontes y algunas como seres humanos.

Cuando nos sale la víbora que llevamos dentro, está en funcionamiento el hipotálamo, un pedazo de cerebro medio escondido debajo del tálamo y encima de la hipófisis; ahí es donde resolvemos nuestras necesidades de frío, de hambre, de sed; donde elaboramos las sensaciones de placer y de dolor; donde decidimos hacer cosas sin pensar y sin saber que hemos decidido hacerlas sin pensar.

Cuando nos sale el rinoceronte que llevamos dentro, está en funcionamiento el sistema límbico, un pedazo de cerebro medio escondido encima del tronco encefálico; ahí es donde aprendemos que es bueno volver sobre lo que nos ha causado placer y huir, olvidar o combatir siempre que algo nos provoca algún daño.

Cuando nos sale el humano, está en funcionamiento el córtex cerebral, un pedazo de cerebro que recubre todos los anteriores y que es más grande que ninguno de ellos; ahí es donde imaginamos víboras sin veneno y rinocerontes que no necesitan llevarse a nadie por delante para estar bien en el mundo.

Los tres cerebros están conectados, los tres actúan a tiempo completo y no siempre están de acuerdo, por eso puede suceder que deseemos lo que no necesitamos, que hagamos lo que no deseamos, que necesitemos lo que no hacemos, o también que no sepamos qué necesitamos, por qué deseamos, ni qué hacer; y entonces todo se vuelve un lío y sólo se nos ocurre callar, dar patadas o escaparnos, con lo fácil que sería ponerse a pensar.

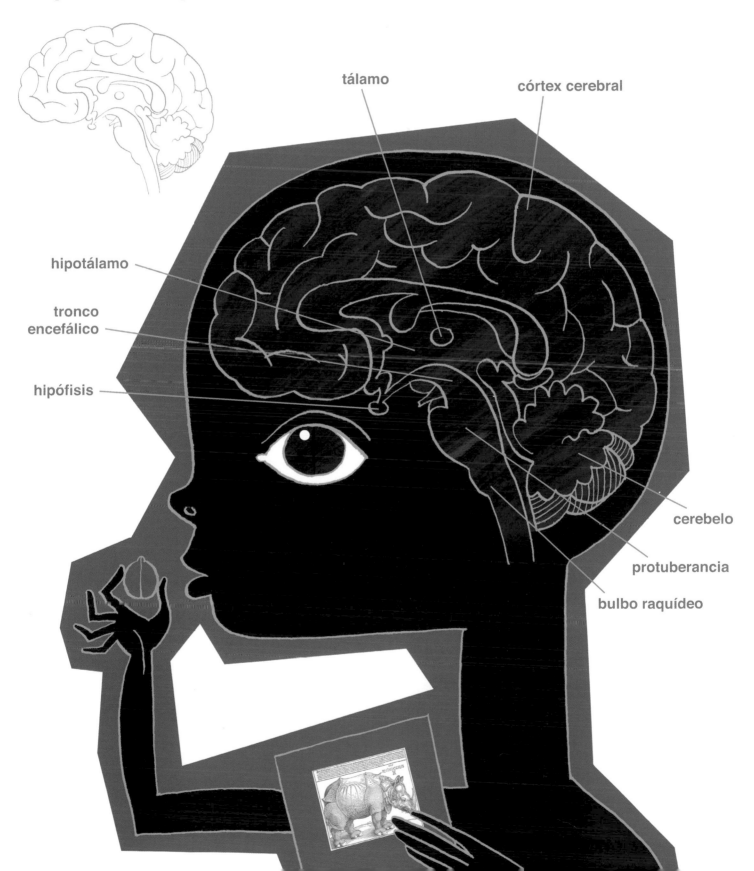

Sistema endocrino

Donde se hace caso a la voz interior

Dormir no es morirse, dormir es quedarse a solas con uno mismo, apartarse durante unos minutos o unas horas del mundo y seguir vivos. Mientras dormimos dejamos de pensar, dejamos de tomar decisiones y dejamos de actuar. Pero no dejamos de respirar y la sangre roja no deja de circular y el pelo largo y el pelo corto no dejan de crecer y los músculos no dejan de moverse vuelta para aquí vuelta para allá. Mientras todo esto sucede, nosotros soñamos con ríos que nunca llegan al mar o con arañas que tienen la voz de alguien conocido.

Mientras dormimos y soñamos, las glándulas no cesan de producir hormonas que se ponen en contacto con otras células o dejan que fluyan por la sangre hasta lugares lejanos. Gracias a esta ocupación lenta y constante podremos despertarnos y reconocer que seguimos siendo nosotros, que yo sigo siendo yo y que tú sigues siendo tú, lo que no quiere decir que sigamos siendo iguales a como éramos, porque para seguir siendo nosotros mismos tenemos que estar siempre cambiando, aunque no nos demos cuenta. No sólo dormidos, también despiertos, de que todo cambie para poder seguir siendo nosotros mismos se ocupan las glándulas y los órganos que conforman el sistema endocrino que, a fin de cuentas, tiene que ver con todas las células de nuestro cuerpo.

Crecemos gracias a que el lóbulo anterior de la glándula pituitaria segrega GH (o somatotropina).

A veces, nos unimos a alguien que deseamos aprovechando que la hipófisis segrega las hormonas LH (o luteinizante) y FSH (o foliculoestimulante).

Podemos huir ante el peligro porque la suprarrenal segrega la hormona noradrenalina.

Dormimos porque tenemos sueño y tenemos sueño porque la pineal segrega la hormona melatonina.

Nos saciamos, vigilamos, cambiamos de voz, ganamos o perdemos pelo, producimos leche, se nos oscurece la piel, retenemos el agua, contraemos el útero, soportamos el frío, nos defendemos de un ataque, y seguimos y seguimos y seguimos porque alguna glándula está haciendo su trabajo, sin anunciarlo, casi en silencio. Sólo cuando logramos a nuestro alrededor un silencio mayor que el silencio de las glándulas podemos escucharlas. Es el mismo sonido del agua en alta mar. Se escucha una única vez en la vida.

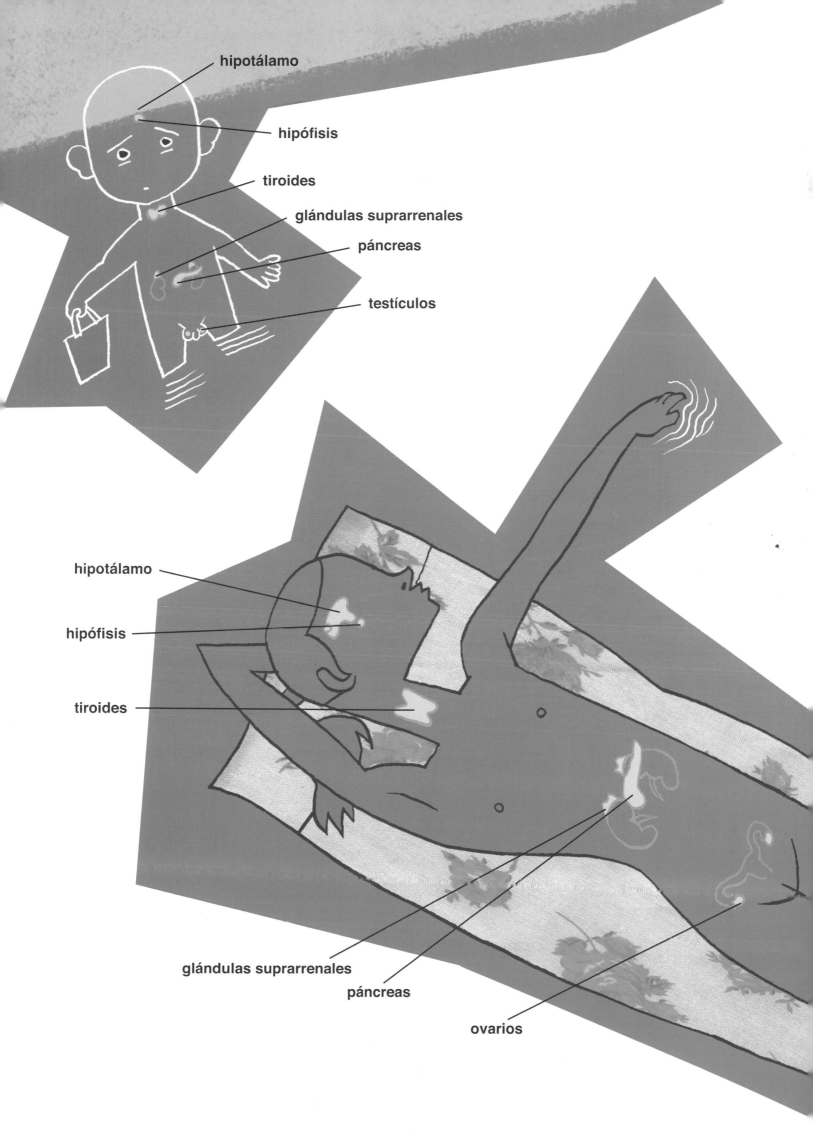

hipotálamo

hipófisis

tiroides

glándulas suprarrenales

páncreas

testículos

hipotálamo

hipófisis

tiroides

glándulas suprarrenales

páncreas

ovarios

CRÁNEO

DONDE SE DESCUBRE QUE LA MUERTE ES OTRA COSA

Dentro del cráneo caben muchas cosas: la mirada, la escucha, el gusto, el olfato, las ideas acertadas, los fracasos, los recuerdos y así simultáneamente.

Los huesos del cráneo, terminada la primera infancia, no se mueven, con esto evitamos que la mirada sobre el mar se confunda con el miedo a los fracasos y el gusto a guayaba no suene al viento atravesando el callejón. Es el cráneo y no el cerebro el que pone cada cosa en su sitio.

Esta inmovilidad tiene una excepción, es excepcional la articulación entre el hueso maxilar inferior y el hueso temporal, que nos permite abrir la boca para cantar, comer, gritar, bostezar, espirar y decir «hace tiempo que no te veía trepar a un árbol».

El cráneo entero sí se mueve: el atlas (la primera vértebra cervical) y el axis (la segunda vértebra cervical) nos permiten mover la cabeza sobre el cuello cuando queremos decir que no, cuando queremos decir que sí, cuando queremos mirar hacia la izquierda porque viene un monstruo de siete vidas, mirar a la derecha porque se ha cerrado una ventana de golpe, mirar hacia abajo para recordar que tenemos pies, y mirar hacia arriba para desear ser un pájaro de esa bandada que se va para no volver.

Debajo de la lengua crece un hueso, sólo hay que buscarlo.

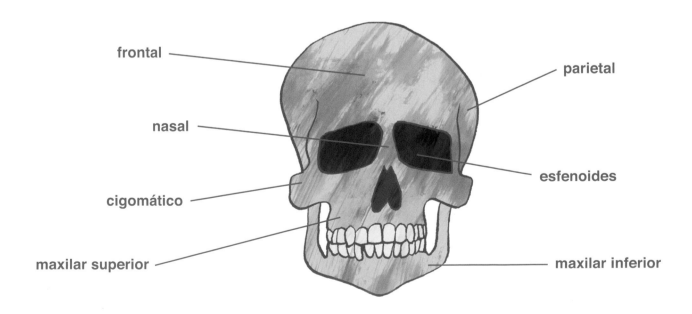

frontal — parietal — nasal — esfenoides — cigomático — maxilar superior — maxilar inferior

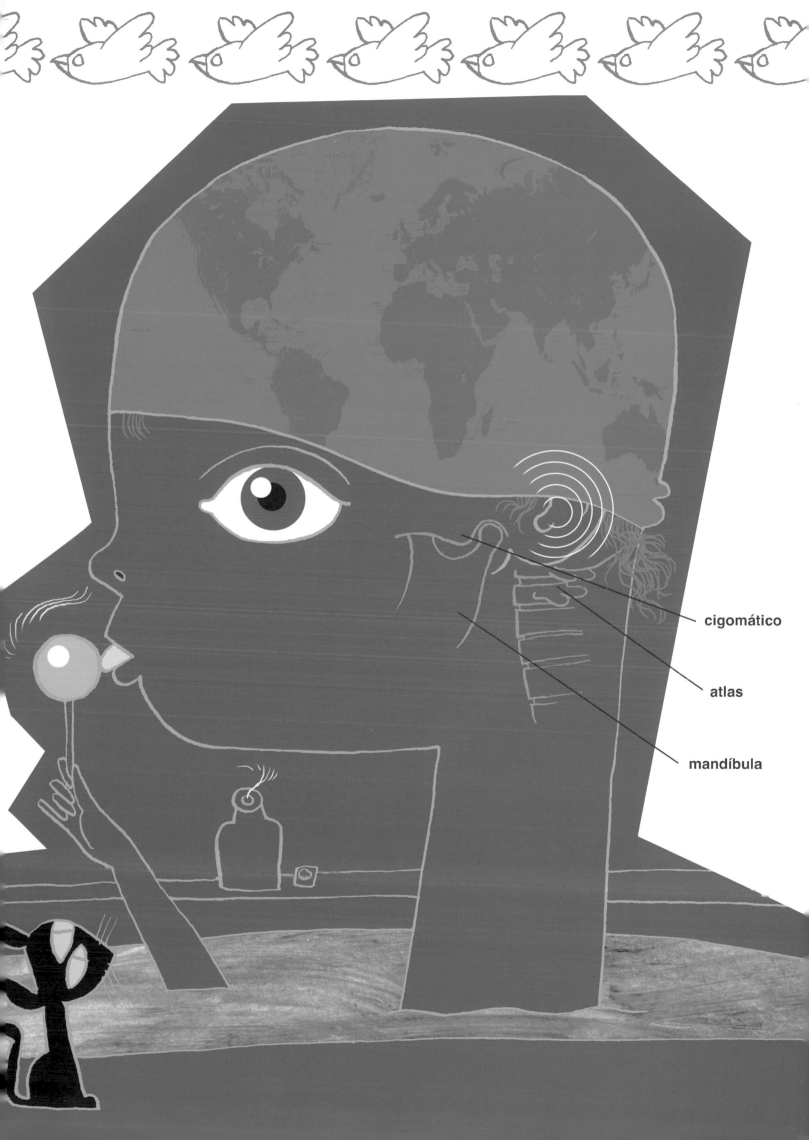

cigomático

atlas

mandíbula

Esqueleto

Donde nos acordamos de dónde venimos y de cómo acabaremos

El esqueleto es un puzle de huesos y articulaciones donde, según la lógica de los puzles, todas las piezas están en su sitio, hasta que se salen de ahí y empieza otra lógica que duele más.

Hay dos tipos de esqueletos: el esqueleto vivo y el esqueleto muerto. El esqueleto muerto siempre se está riendo y cuando intentamos ponerlo de pie, parece que tuviera pasión por el baile; no es así, ha perdido donde apoyarse y se descoyunta. Los esqueletos muertos nos han servido a lo largo de la historia para asustar, para pintar cuadros, para ponernos a pensar en lo desconcertante que es la vanidad y para hacernos una idea de cómo es un esqueleto vivo, porque los esqueletos vivos nunca los vemos, están debajo de los músculos, que están debajo de la piel, que está debajo de la camiseta y el pantalón.

Un esqueleto vivo de una persona adulta tiene 206 huesos; y es probable que sepan a sal.

La primera obligación del esqueleto es mantenernos en equilibrio, no permitir que nos caigamos, hacer todo lo posible por que podamos estar parados cuando lo deseamos, que es muchas más veces de las que recordamos.

La segunda obligación del esqueleto es justo la contraria: permitir movernos por el mundo para conseguir todo lo que necesitamos para seguir vivos.

La tercera obligación del esqueleto es sostener y proteger los órganos internos, el cerebro, los pulmones, el corazón y todo lo demás.

La cuarta obligación del esqueleto es producir dentro de los huesos los elementos necesarios para fabricar sangre.

No es de extrañar que después de haber asumido tantas responsabilidades en vida, al esqueleto muerto le dé por reírse y bailar.

Las obligaciones pesan, el cuerpo también; lo lógico hubiera sido seguir viviendo a cuatro patas, como los monos, los perros, las cabras; sobre cuatro patas el peso está más repartido.

Hubiera sido lógico dentro de la lógica de los pesos. Hay otras lógicas; en la lógica de la evolución, a nuestros antepasados les tocó erguirse poco a poco hasta acabar de pie.

La nueva postura supuso un cambio en la forma de nuestro esqueleto y abrió hueco para que nos creciera más el cerebro, se ampliara la cavidad de la faringe y el dedo pulgar fuera capaz de acariciar los otros cuatro dedos; condiciones que hemos aprovechado para imaginar, hablar y construir toda clase de objetos.

Es posible que con todo ello hayamos aumentado nuestras obligaciones, incluso que ahora tengamos más lógicas que antes, cuando nos sujetábamos sobre cuatro patas, y la vida nos pese más. ¿Qué le vamos a hacer? No lo hemos decidido nosotros.

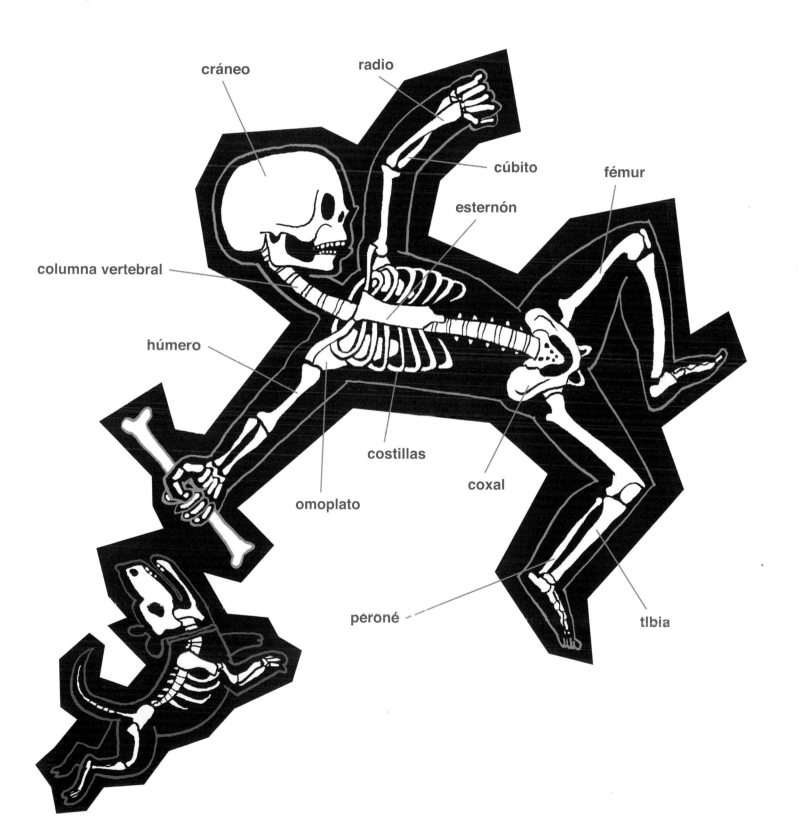

cráneo

radio

cúbito

fémur

esternón

columna vertebral

húmero

costillas

coxal

omoplato

peroné

tlbia

Aparato respiratorio

Donde queda claro que el sol es más importante que la luna, a pesar de lo que digan algunos poetas

El aparato respiratorio se parece mucho a ciertos árboles que se parecen mucho al aparato respiratorio; es posible que nunca hayamos encontrado este parecido porque no estamos acostumbrados a vernos el aparato respiratorio.

Para que el parecido se dé, o los árboles tienen que estar boca abajo o tiene que estar boca abajo el aparato respiratorio; es mucho más fácil lo segundo.

El aparato respiratorio sirve para respirar, respirar sirve para estar vivos. Estar vivos ni sirve ni deja de servir; pero mientras estamos vivos, es mejor estar vivos, por eso respiramos todos los minutos de todas las horas de todos los días de todos los años de nuestra vida. Respirar no es una decisión que tomamos según nuestro estado de ánimo, tampoco es una obligación que pueda acatarse o no, es lo que hay.

Respiramos energía del sol, convertida en planta, convertida en oxígeno.

Como el oxígeno pasa a nuestra sangre, podemos decir que llenamos nuestro cuerpo de pedacitos de sol, o de pedazos, depende de nuestra capacidad pulmonar.

El sol nos lo quedamos y devolvemos anhídrido carbónico. A veces aprovechamos esta devolución para cantar, gemir, silbar, hablar, gritar, hacer ruido.

No siempre, claro; cantar, hablar, silbar o imitar el tictac del reloj antiguo sí que son decisiones y otras veces, muchas veces, decidimos que el aire que devolvemos al aire salga por nuestra nariz o por nuestra boca en silencio, en tanto silencio que entonces nadie se da cuenta de que estamos respirando, nadie, ni nosotros mismos.

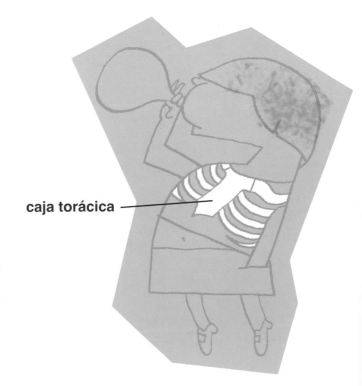

caja torácica

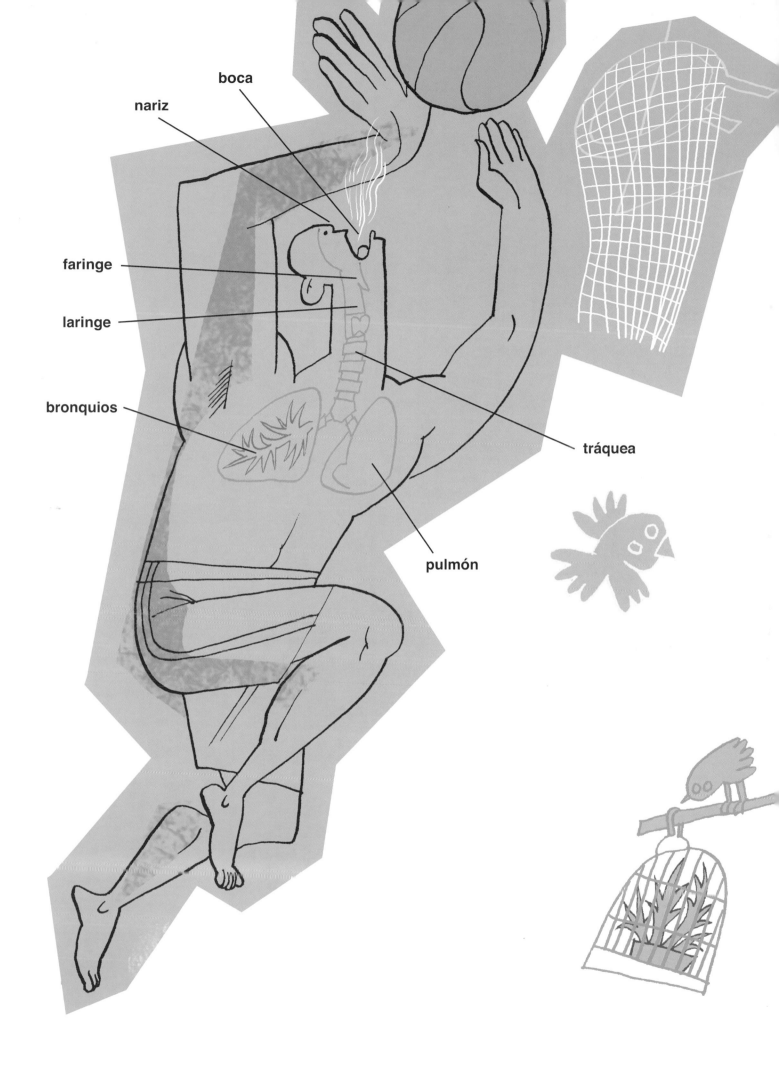

nariz

boca

faringe

laringe

bronquios

tráquea

pulmón

Aparato fonador

Donde se diferencia entre decir y acertar

Las palabras se las lleva el viento. Y las trae. Las palabras son ondas en el aire.

La emisión de voz es una cuestión muscular, resuelta encima de los pulmones, en la que la faringe actúa como caja de resonancia regulada por la posición de la laringe.

Para que las vibraciones de las cuerdas vocales se conviertan en voz no hay que pensar mucho, basta con respirar y tomar alguna decisión: el aire que espiremos a través de la laringe hará vibrar estas fibras. La presión del aire definirá la intensidad del sonido. De la longitud, el grosor y la tensión de las cuerdas vocales dependerá el tono y la tesitura. En la expulsión del aire, la lengua, el paladar blando y los labios diferenciarán nuestro timbre del de otro ser humano.

Al final de este recorrido, la voz que devolvamos al aire será distinta a todas las demás, igual que nuestra cara; y las huellas de nuestros dedos.

Para que la palabra sea la acertada en el momento en el que la pronunciamos sí que hay que pensar mucho. El lenguaje es facultad del sistema nervioso. La voz no es el lenguaje. La voz es animal y humana. El lenguaje sólo es humano.

Con la voz podemos hacer cosas que quizás no podemos hacer con el lenguaje, con el lenguaje podemos hacer cosas que quizás no podemos hacer con la voz.

La memoria es como es, y es bastante animal, por eso muchos de nuestros contemporáneos son capaces de recordar nuestra voz y haber olvidado completamente lo que dijimos.

Será que somos poco más que nuestra voz.

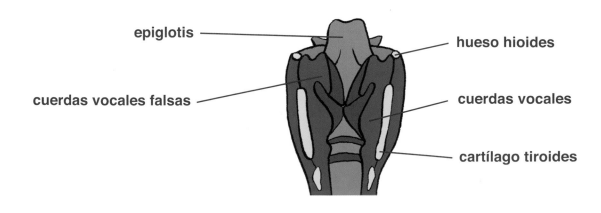

epiglotis

hueso hioides

cuerdas vocales falsas

cuerdas vocales

cartílago tiroides

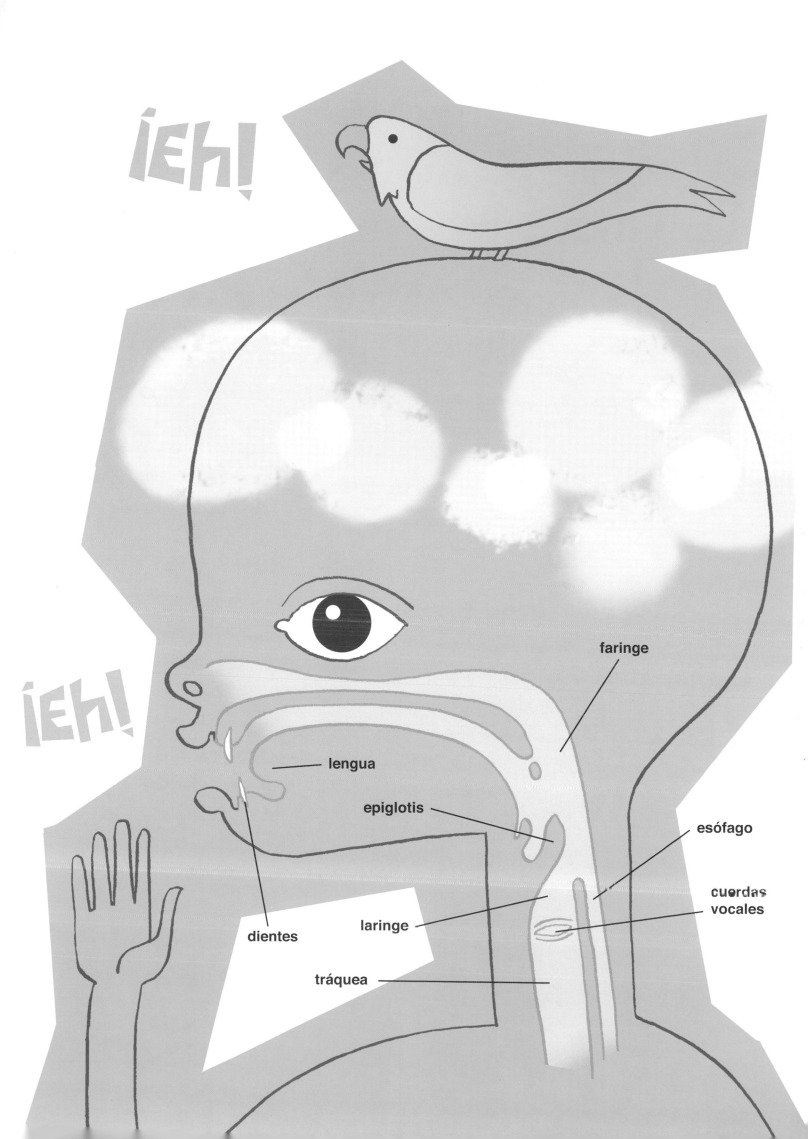

Aparato circulatorio y sistema linfático

Donde se reconoce que todo pende de un hilo

La sangre es roja, la hemos visto salir por la herida y es roja. Alguien nos ha curado, o lo hemos hecho nosotros mismos: la sangre ha dejado de brotar, de desparramarse por la silla, por la alfombra, por las baldosas del mundo y seguimos vivos, seguimos vivos, seguimos vivos. Por eso podemos contarlo.

Cinco o seis litros de sangre roja recorren nuestro cuerpo noche y día, dormidos y despiertos: entran en el corazón, salen del corazón, recorren todo el cuerpo, entran en el corazón, salen del corazón, recorren todo el cuerpo, entran en el corazón, salen del corazón, recorren todo el cuerpo. Todo el cuerpo es todo el cuerpo.

La sangre recorre aproximadamente cien mil kilómetros de arterias y venas para poder llegar a todo el cuerpo. La sangre tiene que llegar hasta el rincón más escondido, más escondido, más escondido, porque si no llega, si algo le impide llegar, si el camino se le vuelve demasiado estrecho o a mitad de recorrido se le cruza un pedazo de nada bueno que no hemos sido capaces de expulsar del cuerpo, esa parte del cuerpo se muere antes de la misma muerte.

La sangre va y viene, va y viene, va y viene siempre por el mismo camino. Otra cosa es que se pierda a borbotones, o con el temblor de un hilo.

La sangre no nace en el corazón; el corazón está hueco.

Es la médula ósea la encargada de fabricar células sanguíneas. La sangre nace en los huesos. De niños, cualquier hueso es bueno para producir sangre; de adultos, son más abundantes los del cráneo, las vértebras, las costillas, la pelvis, el esternón y los fémures.

La médula ósea fabrica glóbulos blancos, monocitos, macrófagos, linfocitos, glóbulos rojos y plaquetas sin cesar; así, aunque la sangre ya no dé más de sí y se destruya en el hígado y en el bazo o se pierda con el temblor de un hilo después de habernos pinchado con la aguja mientras esperábamos la llegada de un amor imposible, siempre podemos disponer de sangre nueva.

Los macrófagos y los linfocitos viajan en la linfa, un fluido que corre por nuestro cuerpo a través de los capilares y los vasos linfáticos. El sistema linfático discurre muy cerca del aparato circulatorio, casi en paralelo, para ir recogiendo lo que no pueden absorber los capilares sanguíneos y las grasas y que no se desperdicie.

Si el sistema linfático no nos perteneciera, pensaríamos que nos quiere una barbaridad, porque siempre está dispuesto a defendernos de elementos extraños, bacterias y células cancerosas. Pero el sistema linfático, con sus ganglios a flor de piel, somos nosotros, así que lo que podemos decir, por decir algo, es que nos queremos mucho.

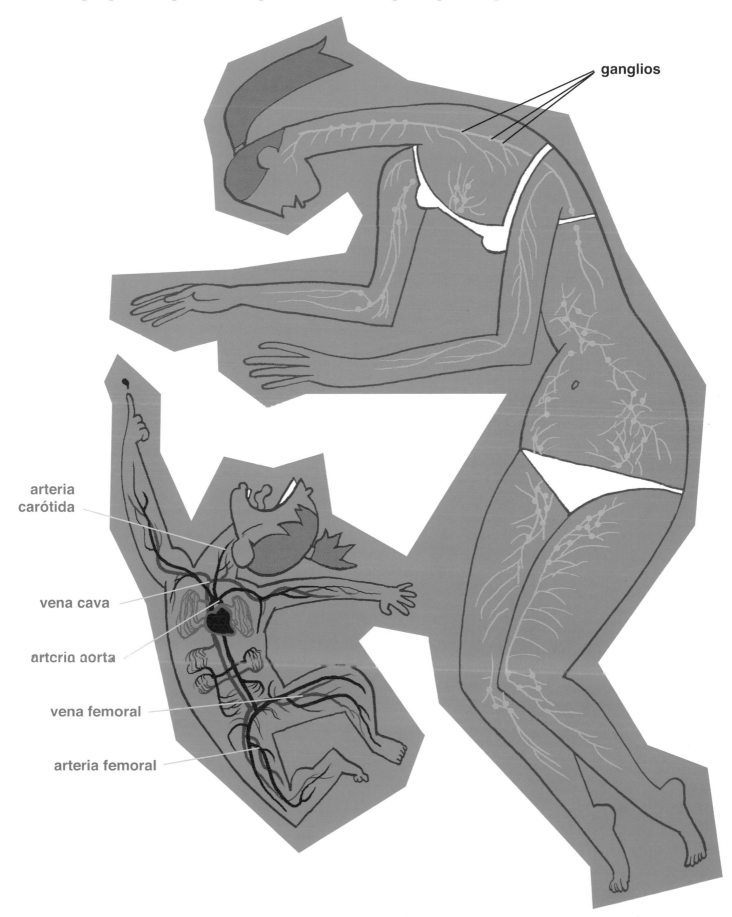

ganglios

arteria carótida

vena cava

arteria aorta

vena femoral

arteria femoral

Corazón

Donde se propone buscar otra ubicación a ciertas pasiones

El amor no nace en el corazón, el corazón es un músculo hueco que se llena y se vacía de sangre, se llena y se vacía de sangre, se llena y se vacía de sangre y que no tiene materia con la que fabricar amor. Tampoco el odio se fabrica en el corazón. Para ver el nacimiento del amor y del odio, como se ve el manantial de algunos ríos entre la espesura de un bosque verde, hay que ir a buscar más arriba.

El corazón de verdad se parece mucho al corazón dibujado. Hay, eso sí, dos diferencias importantes: el corazón de verdad, a diferencia del dibujado, no es plano y casi nunca está atravesado por una flecha.

El corazón de verdad tiene cuatro cavidades, dos aurículas en la parte superior y dos ventrículos en la parte inferior.

Desde el ventrículo izquierdo sale sangre oxigenada por la aorta, una arteria que se va ramificando hasta tejer una red de capilares que entran en contacto con cada punto de tejido de nuestro cuerpo. Esa sangre proporciona oxígeno, agua, alimentos, hormonas y anticuerpos que nos protegen del daño externo; con eso vivimos, con eso vivimos, con eso vivimos.

Los tejidos del cuerpo devuelven a la sangre lo que no necesitan: anhídrido carbónico, sustancias alimenticias, oxígeno, agua; del transporte de esta sangre oscura, casi azul, que regresa por otro camino, se ocupan las venas, que la depositan en la aurícula derecha. Desde ahí, pasará al ventrículo derecho para que éste la envíe al pulmón a purificarse. La sangre que sale oxigenada del pulmón llena la aurícula izquierda antes de pasar al ventrículo izquierdo y volver a empezar, volver a empezar, volver a empezar.

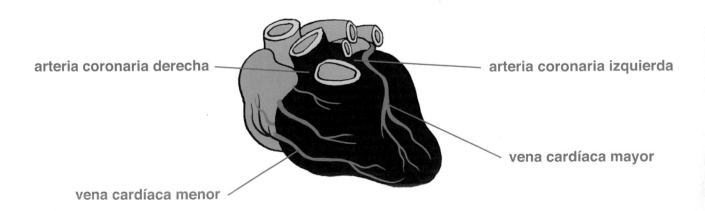

arteria coronaria derecha — — arteria coronaria izquierda

vena cardíaca menor

vena cardíaca mayor

24

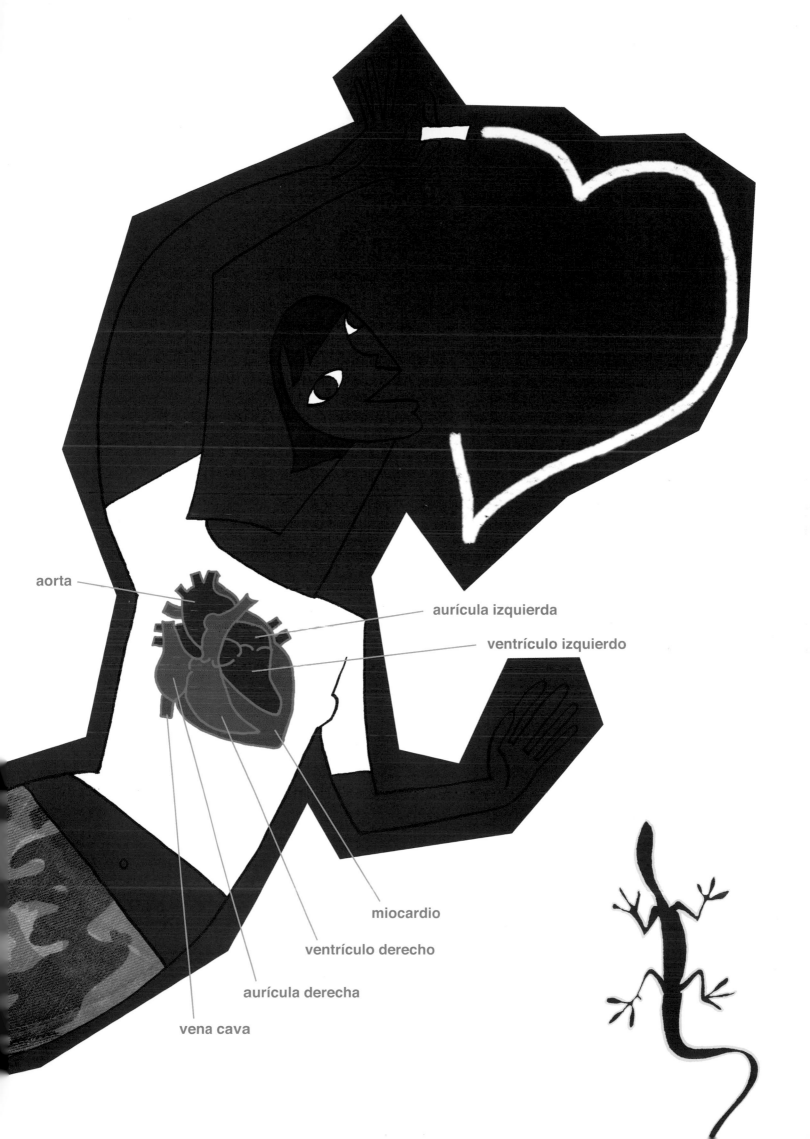

aorta

aurícula izquierda

ventrículo izquierdo

miocardio

ventrículo derecho

aurícula derecha

vena cava

Aparato digestivo

Donde se detalla el recorrido que realizan los pedazos de universo que nos comemos a bocados

El aparato digestivo es una larga sucesión de cavidades, tubos y recipientes que pueden estar llenos o vacíos, como las botellas, las habitaciones o las calles de una ciudad. Para llenarlo tenemos que comer alimentos; para vaciarlo basta con dejarle hacer su trabajo en paz, él se encarga de transportar hasta nuestra sangre lo que necesitamos en cada momento y de expulsar lo que no merece la pena o podría causarnos algún daño.

Que un aparato digestivo esté lleno o vacío no siempre depende de uno: los niños, los náufragos, los presos, los enfermos y los pobres no deciden cuándo comen.

El aparato digestivo consta de boca, lengua, glándulas salivares, faringe, esófago, estómago, intestino delgado, intestino grueso, hígado, vesícula, páncreas y ano.

En el único sitio que hay dientes es en la boca. Si la abrimos, podemos ver qué sucede en el aparato digestivo justo hasta que el alimento llega al istmo de las fauces; desde ahí perdemos de vista la zanahoria que acabamos de morder, masticar y ensalivar. Ahí también, en el istmo de las fauces, en la entrada de la faringe, es donde termina nuestra capacidad de decidir qué va a pasar con la zanahoria, a la que le quedan todavía casi doce metros de recorrido, sola o acompañada, antes de llegar a ser un pedazo de nosotros mismos.

Los jugos gástricos, la bilis, el jugo pancreático, el jugo entérico y la flora bacteriana se hacen cargo, por este orden, de la zanahoria y desencadenan procesos químicos capaces de convertirla en el plazo de unas horas en sangre roja.

Lo que le sucede a la zanahoria dentro del aparato digestivo no es excepcional; todos los alimentos corren la misma suerte. Otra cosa es que uno se meta en la boca un botón, una moneda encontrada en una plaza o un sable. Cuando esto sucede, el aparato digestivo no quiere saber nada y hace lo posible por quitarse de encima lo antes posible el objeto intruso.

El aparato digestivo empieza en un agujero y termina en otro agujero como no podía ser de otra manera: no todos los trozos de realidad que nos comemos nos son de provecho. El intestino grueso termina en el recto y el recto se abre al mundo a través del ano. Lo que empezó por delante, termina por detrás, el cuerpo tiene dos caras.

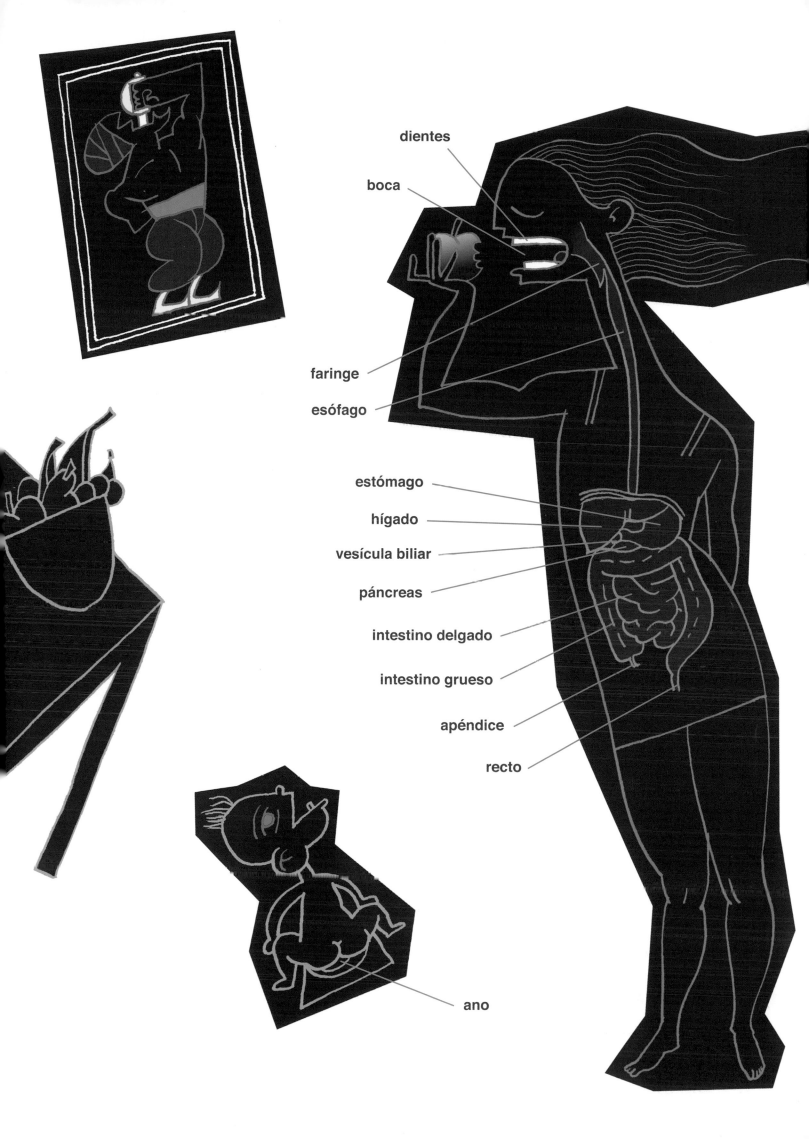

dientes

boca

faringe

esófago

estómago

hígado

vesícula biliar

páncreas

intestino delgado

intestino grueso

apéndice

recto

ano

Aparato urinario

Donde se trata del beneficio de la meada

La orina no es lo que parece, ni siquiera es aceite de girasol, mucho menos caldo de verduras. No hay que empeñarse. El limón, las pipas de girasol, las alcachofas, la trucha (más la espina cuando nos la hemos tragado sin darnos cuenta) y todo lo que comemos y bebemos, cuando está dentro de nuestro cuerpo deja de ser lo que era encima de la mesa y acaba siendo azúcares, ácidos grasos, aminoácidos, agua, sales minerales, vitaminas, materia que sí puede pasar a la sangre y de la sangre a las células. Por eso cuando nos hacemos una herida en el dedo y corre la sangre como si fuera el fin del mundo, no aparecen rodajas de berenjena ni hojas de lechuga; en la sangre ya no hay berenjena.

Entre tanto pasar de ser pollo a ser aminoácido, o convertirse la manzana reineta en vitamina, vamos creando dentro de nuestro cuerpo sustancias inútiles o que abundan tanto que sobran o que, decididamente, no nos hacen ningún bien: agua, algo de cloruro sódico y de urea y una pizca de ácido úrico y de fosfatos y sulfatos, ingredientes con los que los riñones fabrican orina, que no es lo que parece.

Riñones tenemos dos, como codos, que también tenemos dos. Si dejamos colgar los brazos, los codos nos quedan a la altura de los riñones. Un riñón es más grande que un codo y más blando, lo que no quiere decir que sea menos resistente.

A los riñones les llega sangre a través de la arteria renal. En esa sangre hay de todo, o de casi todo. Un millón de nefrones está dispuesto en cada riñón para separar lo que de esa sangre nos sirve de lo que no nos sirve. Lo que sirve vuelve a la sangre por la vena renal hasta la vena cava. Lo que no sirve se evacua por los uréteres hasta la vejiga. Los riñones son fabricantes de orina y de equilibrio homeostático, la orina es más fácil de ver que el equilibrio homeostático.

En la vejiga cabe lo que cabe y cuando no cabe más, toda esta materia en estado líquido, de color claro, a veces más brillante y en ocasiones profundamente olorosa, que no es lo que parece, acaba volviendo al mundo a través de la uretra, un vaso que llega hasta el extremo del pene en el hombre y que desemboca en la vulva de la mujer por delante del orificio externo de la vagina.

Los seres humanos orinamos a menudo y sin pensarlo mucho: 10.500.000.000.000 litros de orina por día en el mundo, entre todos, aproximadamente. Un enorme lago, un mar pequeñito y dorado. Con los años aprendemos a controlar nuestra vejiga, a decidir cuándo la vaciamos. Este aprendizaje no nos sirve de nada cuando aparecen la risa o el miedo. Cuando nos morimos de risa o de miedo, nos orinamos. Cuando nos morimos para siempre, a veces también nos orinamos.

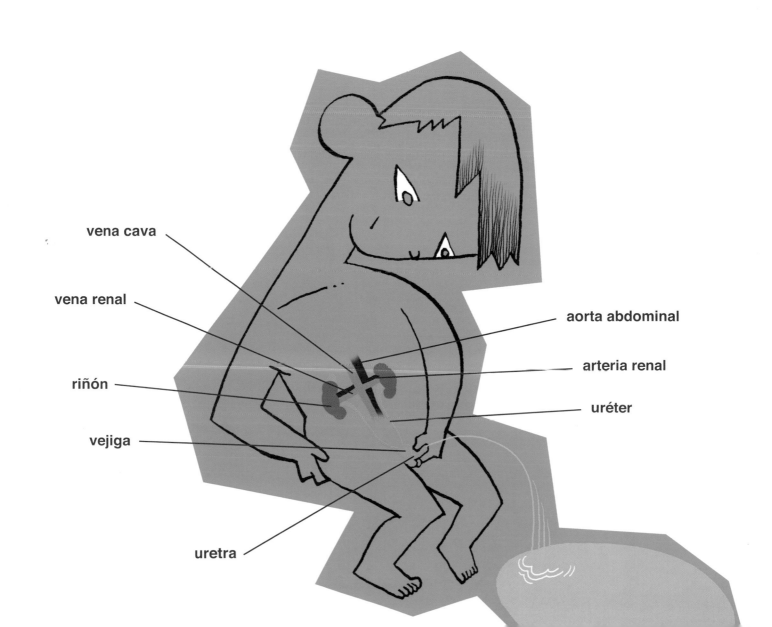

Pelo

Donde se concibe que la necesidad pueda acabar en adorno

El pelo, un pelo, muchos pelos, el pelo. ¿Tenemos un pelo o pelo? Poco importa: el pelo es una enorme cantidad de un pelo y otro pelo, pura proteína con forma de hélice girando hacia la derecha: la queratina. Con la queratina los pájaros se fabrican plumas, las vacas cuernos, las ovejas lana y la tortuga su caparazón.

La queratina se sintetiza en el folículo, dentro de la piel, en el nacimiento del pelo; algo más arriba, la melanina lo tiñe de moreno o la *phéomelanina* lo tiñe de rubio o rojo. Son los colores del pelo

Cuando el pelo sale del folículo, una glándula segrega el sebo que lo engrasará. Una vez fuera de la piel, el pelo sigue creciendo.

Tenemos millones de pelos en la piel. Y tenemos millones de pelos dentro del cuerpo, a los de dentro no les hacemos tanto caso.

En las palmas de las manos y en las plantas de los pies no tenemos pelo; en el resto del cuerpo, puede aparecer por cualquier lado. El pelo de la cabeza es el más famoso; es tan famoso que se sigue hablando de él cuando ha desaparecido: no hay calvo que no se acuerde de su perdida cabellera en alguna conversación.

El pelo de las pestañas también está bien visto, por los otros, claro, y a veces el de la cara, que ha conseguido tener nombre propio, llamarse barba y bigote. El pelo de las cejas, de las orejas, de la nariz, del pecho, de la espalda, de las nalgas, de la vulva, del escroto, de las piernas y de los pies corre distinta suerte según la manera de entender la vida del humano al que le crece.

El pelo no duele, quizás por eso no nos cuesta nada arrancarlo, cortarlo, afeitarlo, pintarlo de colores distintos a los colores del pelo, rizarlo cuando es liso y ali-

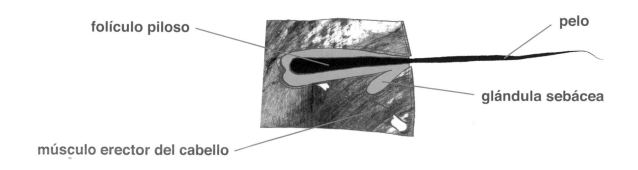

folículo piloso

músculo erector del cabello

pelo

glándula sebácea

sarlo cuando es rizado o crespo. Con todos estos tejemanejes buscamos la belleza. La belleza es una invención, como la cafetera o el fin de semana.

El pelo no duele, pero siente; siente el calor, el frío, el placer, el miedo, y responde a la sensación bien relajándose hasta recostarse sobre nuestra piel, bien erizándose. Mientras se nos sigan poniendo los pelos de punta porque sí o porque no, será señal de que estamos vivos. Las calaveras son calvas.

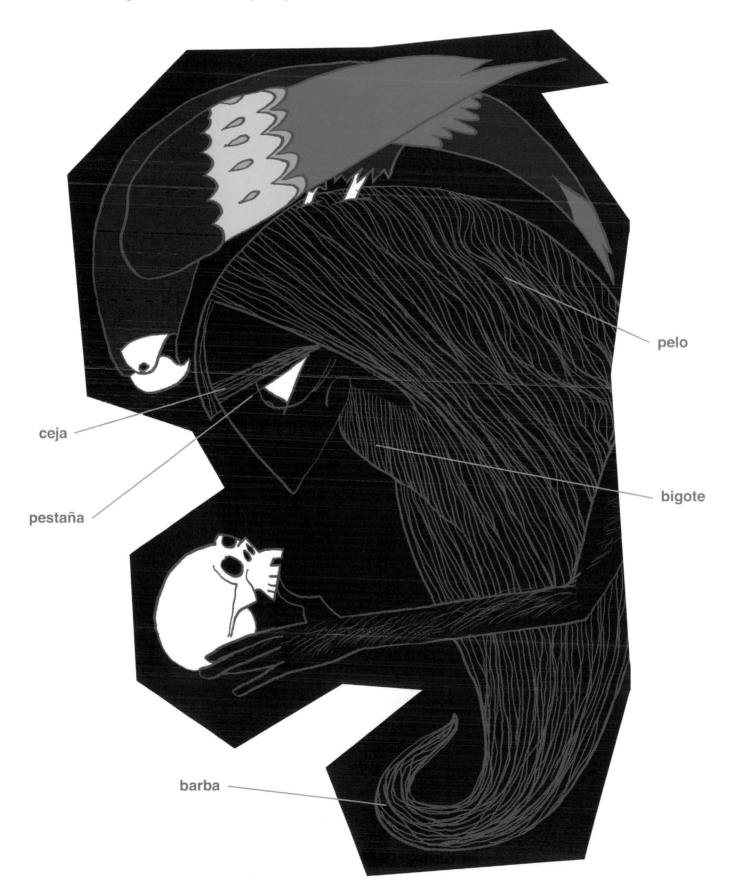

pelo

ceja

bigote

pestaña

barba

SISTEMA MUSCULAR

DONDE SE CONCLUYE QUE NO HAY QUE FIARSE DE LA PRIMERA IMPRESIÓN

No paramos.

Aunque nos quedemos inmóviles en una esquina de una calle larga, con los pies clavados en el suelo y sin pestañear, y no saquemos las manos de los bolsillos y no volvamos la cabeza y no abramos la boca, seguiremos en movimiento.

El simpático y el parasimpático estarán actuando sin pausa, a su ritmo, para enviar impulsos nerviosos al músculo cardiaco y a los músculos lisos que se encargarán de que no cesen los movimientos del corazón, la pupila, las glándulas salivares, los pulmones, el estómago, el intestino, las glándulas suprarrenales y la vejiga. Pasará alguien a nuestro lado y no caerá en la cuenta, creerá que estamos quietos. Ni siquiera si es un conocido nuestro, un amigo, reparará en el hecho.

Otra cosa será si desde el sistema nervioso central decidimos dar paraditas contra la acera, brincar o ponernos a bailar en esa misma esquina. Si nos atrevemos, más de 650 músculos empezarán a contraerse y a distenderse para que el esqueleto pueda moverse y nosotros podamos bailar. Entonces, todo el barrio se enterará de que estamos bailando y alguien se contagiará y se pondrá a bailar junto a nosotros, y si esto sucede, es probable que sigamos un rato más de lo que teníamos pensado. Hasta que nos cansemos y no podamos seguir.

Nos cansamos porque en los esfuerzos, el músculo consume energía y en toda producción de energía queda resto de algo que no sirve para nada bueno. Mientras la cantidad de desechos es poca, la sangre tiene tiempo de irlos sacando del músculo y de llevarlos donde poder expulsarlos del cuerpo; cuando continuamos haciendo esfuerzo y produciendo energía y generando deshechos, la sangre no puede con todo y nosotros nos venimos abajo, que es una de las formas que tenemos de descansar.

En ese decisivo instante, volveremos a esa posición que no pero que sí, a la quietud en perpetuo movimiento, a la misma esquina. Los músculos tienen tendencia a volver al lugar de donde partieron.

Y allí, con las manos en los bolsillos, sin pestañear, los pies clavados en el suelo nos pondremos a repetir esterno-cleidomastoideo, esternocleidomastoideo, esternocleidomastoideo, esternocleido-mastoideo, esternocleidomastoideo, es-ternocleidomastoideo, esternocleidomas-toideo, esternocleidomastoideo, esterno-cleidomastoideo…, exagerando el gesto, deteniéndonos en cada sílaba, creyéndo-nos que repetir esternocleidomastoideo en la esquina del barrio y ser feliz son los dos mejores antídotos contra las arrugas de la cara.

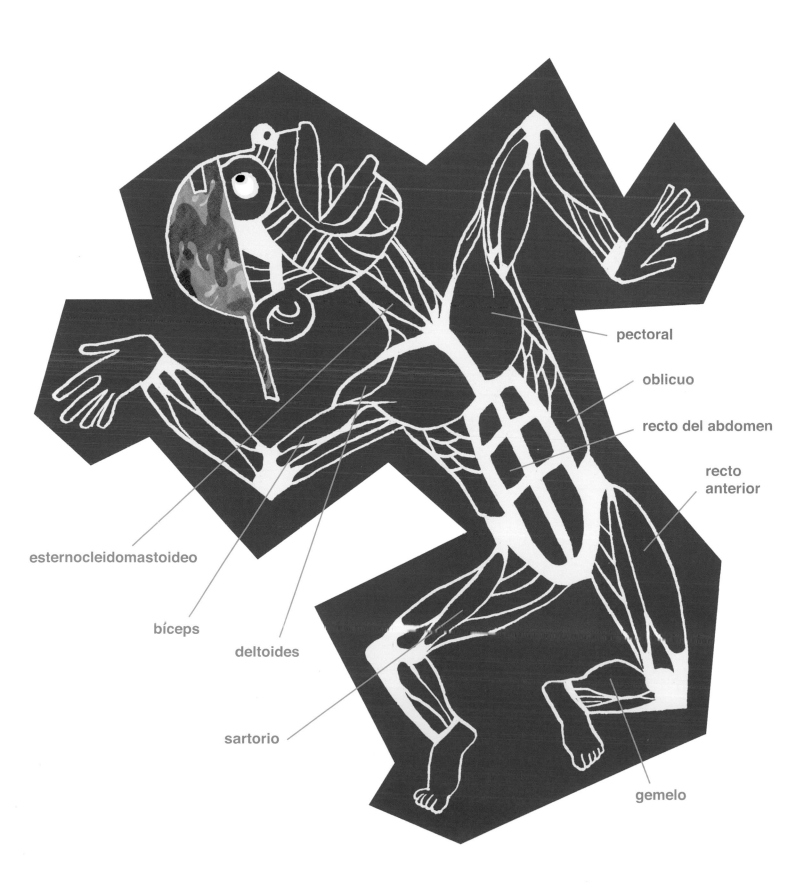

pectoral

oblicuo

recto del abdomen

recto
anterior

esternocleidomastoideo

bíceps

deltoides

sartorio

gemelo

MANOS

DONDE EL FINAL Y EL PRINCIPIO SE JUNTAN

No somos los únicos seres vivos que podemos agarrar cosas con las manos, pero somos los únicos que vamos de un sitio a otro sin parar y que no tenemos que soltar las cosas cuando vamos de un sitio a otro, esta diferencia nos ha separado definitivamente del resto de especies animales. Los veintisiete huesecillos y las varias decenas de músculos y tendones que cuelgan de nuestros brazos nos han hecho humanos.

Cuando el mono bajó del árbol y empezó a liberar sus patas delanteras de la obligación de soportar el peso y el movimiento de su cuerpo, las manos empezaron a evolucionar con un único fin: fabricar utensilios que le permitieran al-mono-que-iba-para-humano obtener alimentos que hasta entonces no había podido disfrutar. El mundo ya no se acababa en la copa de los árboles del lugar que le había visto nacer y la diversificación de alimentos podía evitarle la competencia entre especies, incluso apoderarse de otras especies en beneficio propio.

Y no sólo se trataba de obtener los alimentos, sino de adaptarlos a sus capacidades de gusto, masticación y digestión mediante el arte de la cocina. El mono-que-iba-a-ser-humano fue cocinero antes que fraile, rey, filósofo, artista o científico.

Si más tarde llegó a tener alguna de estas ocupaciones u otras igual de humanas fue porque mientras seguía cocinando o cultivando con sus dos manos, descubrió que los gritos no eran ya suficientes para las novedades que tenía que contar a sus semejantes y aprovechó que el cráneo empezaba a erguirse sobre la columna vertebral y que el aparato fonador permitía matices inauditos a su voz, para empezar a hablar con palabras. Las palabras le descubrieron que el mundo no se acababa en el límite que abarcaban sus sentidos y que era posible ponerse a pensar. Para entonces el cráneo ya había dejado libre el espacio que el cerebro necesitaba para tener ideas que nunca antes había tenido. Así fue como el-mono-que-iba-para-humano llegó, a través de cientos de millones de años, a ser humano-con-memoria-de-mono.

Eso somos, memoria de mono, memoria de lagartija, memoria de nosotros mismos.

Este libro está a punto de acabar, le quedan muy pocas páginas, y es ahora cuando caemos en la cuenta de que las manos que lo han escrito, las manos que lo han dibujado, las que lo han impreso, las que lo han transportado, las que lo han ofrecido, las que lo han mantenido alzado durante la lectura, las que han pasado hoja a hoja, las que lo cerrarán dentro de unos segundos, todas ellas se parecen mucho, muchísimo, a las manos del animal que por primera vez en la historia de la evolución metió un pescado en agua hirviendo y se lo comió.

Ahí empezó el lío.

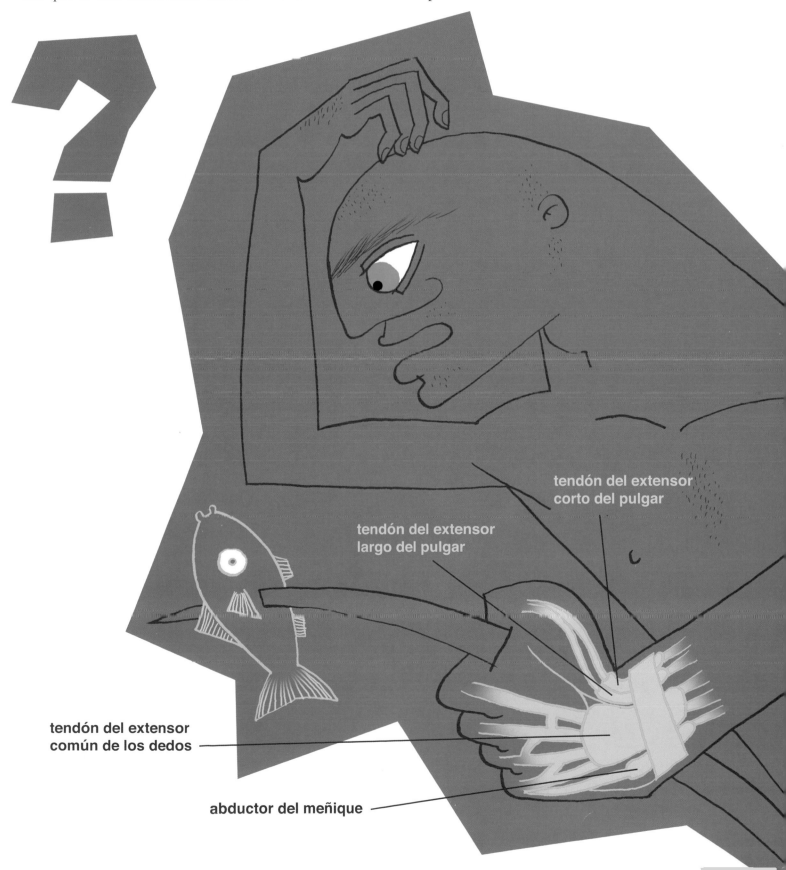

tendón del extensor corto del pulgar

tendón del extensor largo del pulgar

tendón del extensor común de los dedos

abductor del meñique

Higiene y curiosidades

De los órganos genitales

- La lengua, la hipófisis y las pestañas, entre otras partes del cuerpo, también son sexuales.
- A los órganos genitales les sientan mal las mentiras y la oscuridad prolongada.

Del sistema nervioso

- El sistema nervioso es el de la curiosidad: todo le atrae, todo le interesa, se entera de todo (cuando puede).
- Las células tienen información. El sistema nervioso y las hormonas distribuyen esa información por todo el cuerpo. La información es información y no es ni hueso, ni sangre, ni tejido, ni masa, ni energía.
- Al sistema nervioso le sientan mal quedarse con las ganas de hacer algo y las voces que dan los que no tienen razón.

Del cerebro

- Definición: un ser humano es un ser contradictorio.

- Vaciar el cerebro se llama descerebramiento y es una costumbre antigua.
- La lista de lo que le sienta mal al cerebro es enorme y quizás no le sentara bien al cerebro conocerla entera de golpe; anotaremos algunas circunstancias elegidas al azar. Al cerebro le sientan mal la falta de sueño, la soledad, la rutina, los tópicos y comer algunas carnes mientras se decide sobre la vida de algún semejante.

Del sistema endocrino

- Al sistema endocrino le sienta mal el desequilibrio.
- Sólo se habla de las hormonas cuando truena.
- El cerebro es una glándula.

Del cráneo

- Cuando el cráneo pierde el sombrero y luego pierde el pelo y más tarde pierde la piel y al fin pierde los músculos, queda en calavera monda y lironda.
- Una calavera no es la muerte; la muerte es otra cosa. Esto es una verdad.

- Otra verdad es que ningún niño tiene la cabeza dura, por más que se lo repitan sus padres.
- Al cráneo le sienta mal la guillotina.

DEL ESQUELETO

- La columna vertebral es tan importante que a muchas cosas importantes las llamamos columna vertebral aunque no lo sean. Así se construyen las metáforas.
- Un hueso puede romperse de ocho maneras diferentes. En ese instante, recordamos que tenemos esqueleto. El dolor siempre nos trae cosas a la memoria.
- Lo último que desaparece de nosotros después de morir son los huesos. Los huesos son como las piedras del río; cuando el río se seca, las piedras siguen ahí.
- Al esqueleto le sientan mal no tener dónde ir y la tortura.

DEL APARATO RESPIRATORIO

- Los pulmones están dentro de la caja torácica; la caja torácica se parece demasiado a una jaula. Si el aparato respiratorio no estuviera encerrado en la caja torácica que se parece demasiado a una jaula, los pájaros volarían hasta él para construir nidos y a los poetas les haría gracia.
- Al aparato respiratorio le sientan mal el progreso y los días de niebla.

DEL APARATO FONADOR

- El silencio no existe.
- Cuando hablamos con la voz interior las cuerdas vocales también vibran.
- Al aparato fonador le sientan mal el frío, los lugares comunes y la censura.

DEL APARATO CIRCULATORIO Y EL SISTEMA LINFÁTICO

- A veces, la sangre se acumula en alguna parte de nuestro cuerpo para bien. Otra veces, no.
- Los cobardes también tienen sangre en las venas.
- Diderot estaba convencido de que la melancolía se aloja en el bazo.
- Al sistema linfático le sienta mal el desconocimiento.
- Al aparato circulatorio le sientan mal que pase mucho tiempo y que haya poco espacio.

DEL CORAZÓN

- No somos ni más ni menos humanos por tener corazón. Que le pregunten al lagarto.
- El corazón sabe qué es el miedo.
- Podemos vivir con la sangre de otra persona, con el corazón de otra persona, pero no podemos vivir con la memoria de otra persona. El corazón no se acuerda de nada.

- Al corazón le sientan mal los malos humos y las despedidas.

DEL APARATO DIGESTIVO

- El aparato digestivo es el precursor del reloj de pared.
- No es lo mismo digerir que tragar.
- Al aparato digestivo le sientan mal las penas, los venenos y el hambre.

DEL APARATO URINARIO

- Al aparato urinario le sienta mal tener que pedir permiso.

DEL PELO

- Se dice horripilante y está bien dicho.
- Hay quien tiene miedo del pelo. Hay quien tiene miedo de que le corten el pelo. Son miedos distintos.

- El arsénico es un veneno. Los pelos contienen arsénico, pero no en cantidad suficiente para envenenar. Un pelo en el café con leche no acaba con la vida de nadie; quizás acabe con la paciencia.
- Al pelo le sientan mal las discusiones y algunos sustos.

DEL SISTEMA MUSCULAR

- A los músculos les sientan mal los concursos de músculos y trabajar para el amo.
- Los músculos también están formados por células.
- De la vida de los músculos saben mucho los huesos, los nervios y algunas hormonas.

DE LAS MANOS

- A las manos les sienta mal no tener nada que hacer. Fin.

ÍNDICE

Durante
todo el día
que se llamó 16 de enero de 2008
nacieron más seres humanos de los que perecieron;
así viene pasando desde que somos capaces de contar.
Ese día 16 de enero de 2008
se acabó de imprimir
en la lejana China
este libro
titulado
Este cuerpo es humano.
¡Qué coincidencia!